THE PENCE

PRINCIPLE

Lessons All Men Must Learn from Ford-Kavanaugh

Randall Bentwick

TABLE OF CONTENTS

CHAPTER 1
WHO'S LAUGHING NOW?

On March 28th, 2017 an article was written by one Ashley Parker of *The Washington Post*. It was a profile piece on Karen Pence, the wife of the recently-inaugurated Vice President, Mike Pence. It covered their relationship, how they met, the various roles she played in supporting her husband, and their religion. But the one bit of information that was focused on more than anything else was a policy Vice President Pence had followed since they were married:

He would never dine alone with another woman, or attend parties where alcohol was being served, without the presence of his betrothed.

The response was speculative and salacious as much as it was fierce and divisive.

Did Mike Pence not trust women?
Did Mrs. Pence not trust her husband?
Was the Vice President being just an outdated, overly-Christian prude?
Or was he just madly in love with his wife?
Perhaps he was an alcoholic?
Or perhaps an incident involving alcohol and other women resulted in this policy?

Regardless of the true reason, the media and mainstream settled on the narrative that the Vice President was an old, outdated, fuddy-duddy. An overly-worried Christian, hopelessly out of touch with the progressive new world. An archaic sexist whose antiquated views proved women were oppressed, and at the highest levels of government no less. Still, the news story ran its expected lifespan, it dropped out of the headlines, Americans found a new shiny object, and Mike Pence's policy to only dine with his wife became an interesting, quirky footnote in his Wikipedia entry.

That is until September 16th, 2018.

Because on that day one Christine Blasey Ford stepped into the political spotlight, accused President Trump's Supreme Court Justice nominee, Brett Kavanaugh, of sexual assault and threw the nomination procedure into complete and utter chaos.

The drama that would ensue would dwarf the previous record for judicial nomination drama held by the Clarence Thomas nomination some 27 years earlier. Though a simple case of "he said she said," the Democrat Party, desperate to keep a conservative off the Supreme Court, pulled out all the stops in the hopes of delaying a vote until they could potentially win the Senate in the 2018 midterm elections. This resulted in a free-for-all where common sense, intellectual honesty, procedure, decency, and even law were thrown out the window for political purposes.

Additional women came out of the woodwork with equally dubious accusations against Kavanaugh hailing from the 1980's. No witnesses could be found who could corroborate any of their claims, let alone Mrs. Ford's. Some of their claims amounted to nothing more than "I saw him drinking a lot at a party once." Their political motivations were plainly obvious, with most being registered Democrats and working in colleges, social work, and other political "activist" type professions. And the timing of these accusations made it painfully clear that their motive was not noble, but political. To any independent observer it was very clear what these women were doing. And to anybody with a soul, they were disgusted by how they were destroying an innocent man for attention and political gain. But what's worse is this was the *sane part* of this judicial soap opera, as we were about to go into the Twilight Zone.

Soon *high school yearbook entries* were being scoured by the media for insight into Kavanaugh's "partying lifestyle." Any Dick and Tom was given media coverage if they claimed they knew something about Kavanaugh. I personally saw a headline on cable news that unbelievably said, "Kavanaugh's College Drinking Under Scrutiny." And if you didn't believe the media had a horse in this race or was completely biased, some journalist went to the extent to find out that Brett Kavanaugh...

threw some ice at somebody...
in a bar...
in 1985...
and thought it was worth publishing.

If you thought it couldn't get any worse, it did: a significant percent of the American population actually believed the spurious claims of Kavanaugh's accusers and the Democrat Party. However, it is not so much that polls showed roughly one-third of the American public believed Mrs. Ford, as much as it was their shocking disregard for due process, due diligence, the presumption of innocence, and their desire to deny a private citizen those rights. They had no desire or demand for evidence or proof, just a blind faith encapsulated by the mantra "Believe Women" This resulted in a political cult-mob fueled by emotion, gender politics, and hate completely untethered from reality, law, or ethics. And when it came to choosing blind politics over the rights of individual citizens, law, and simple reality, these sheep blindingly choose tyranny and oppression. Temper tantrums flared as these people held protests across the nation. Hundreds were arrested and jailed not knowing they were advocating tyranny. And though millions across the nation were protesting Kavanaugh's nomination, perhaps the epitome of how tyrannical and feral these people were was a video by one Charlie Kirk where protestors (against Kavanaugh) made it perfectly clear they had no desire to adhere to the presumption of innocence, due process, or due diligence. Their politics were more important than democracy, the nation, the law, and individual rights (https://www.youtube.com/watch?v=BkATgD7I_Qo).

For people involved in Washington politics this train wreck may have just been another day at the office. For those who are politically active or are professional activists themselves, their duty or calling. And for journalists who make a living, digging in the mire and muck of politics, normal. But for the American people, it was having their eyes raped.

What the professional politicians, journalist-pundits, and braindead protestors didn't realize was the rest of the world was watching. And whether people are Democrats or Republicans, Conservatives or Liberals, Progressives or Traditionalists, they're not low-life politicians, activists, or journalists. They like things like "proof," "evidence," the "presumption of innocence," "law," "individual rights," and "democracy." But with due process, due diligence, and the presumption of innocence being thrown out the window, normal American citizens were seeing tyranny, corrupt politics, hate, and just plain insanity unfold before their very eyes.

You're going to accuse a guy of sexual harassment from 36 years ago?
You're going to do it now, right before he's nominated to the Supreme Court?
You're going to scour a man's high school yearbook entries?
You're going to criminalize and destroy a person's life because of underage drinking?
You're going to throw a communal temper tantrum because people dare ask for evidence and proof of guilt?

And you're going to demand we blindly believe women when it plainly comes at the expense of a man?

Do not tell the American people you were doing this for them. This was nothing more than a vile and disgusting witch hunt.

There is, however, one unfortunate technicality.

This wasn't a witch hunt. It was a warlock hunt. Because it was a man getting dragged through the streets by women who (in all likelihood) lied about their sexual assaults. And do not think this was a one-time event, relegated to the unfortunate soul of Brett Kavanaugh. The exact same thing happened 27 years earlier to Judge Clarence Thomas, continues today and will continue into the future. It is an epidemic and a trend, and it shows no signs of stopping.

So remember how you all rolled your eyes when Vice President Pence said he refuses to dine alone with other women? Remember how you scoffed at his ole Christian fuddy-duddery and prudishness? Remember how some of you even called him sexist for having such a policy?

Well guess who's laughing now.

An Unfortunate Reality

The Ford-Kavanaugh debacle is merely the most recent and most profiled event of a much larger and dangerous trend. Even considering the microscopic chance Kavanaugh's accusers were telling the truth, it is the metaphorical "tip of the iceberg." And while many of you will dismiss this as conspiracy theory or outlandish politics, need I remind you of the crater where Brett Kavanaugh once stood and the now-vindicated wisdom of Vice President Pence?

This trend is simply the weaponization of women and the criminalization of men. Even more simply put, the hatred of men. On the face of it, it may not make any sense to simply "hate men," but there is much to be gained by jumping on this bandwagon. Political power, financial gain, easier lives, preferential treatment, even something as sad and pathetic as mere attention. All of this can be gained by propagating the façade of an oppressor class and a victim class. And if women (or any group of people in theory) can portray themselves as the victim, they can make the political case and argument for special treatment, compensation, favorable laws, lower standards, income transfers, and a whole host of other benefits.

Admittedly, this is a VERY abbreviated version of what is going on, as well as an audacious claim. But do not be fooled. There ARE women that hate you. There ARE women being brainwashed right now to view you as the enemy. There ARE women fully indoctrinated to ruin your life if it advances theirs. And while thankfully it is not the majority of women, and there are loving, caring women who do love you, it only takes one mentally ill and sick torpedo to sink a ship. The question is: can you afford to take that risk? And the answer is you can't.

Millions of men will spend trillions of hours slaving and toiling to build lives. They will go to school for decades, spend decades more in a career or profession. They will invest in themselves and their futures. They will find love and invest in their wives and their children, and they will invest in their communities and society. They will not have one single ounce of ill-will or bigotry against women, but if they offend the forever-increasingly fragile sensibilities of a weaponized woman, make an awkward pass at a professional victim, or they merely rise through the societal ranks to a position of power, they and their lives become a target for opportunistic destruction by these vile and evil women.

Every young boy, father, and old man needs a wake-up call to this present, increasing, and very real threat. Everything you worked for, and will continue to work for, for your entire life is at risk. Everything you love can be taken away from you. This handbook is a regrettable mandatory insurance policy every man must read. But it can save your life if you follow The Pence Principle.

CHAPTER 2
THE THREAT IS REAL

Origins

While the trend of weaponized women using false claims of victimhood to extract money, resources, and attention from innocent men is a relatively recent event in the grand expanse of human evolution, the threat of theft and personal destruction has always been a part of human nature. The day we genetically separated ourselves from the apes, humans have pursued a strategy of theft, parasitism, and opportunistic destruction as a survival and advancement strategy. This didn't make it moral, and certainly presented a hurdle to the development of civilized society, but it is a tempting part of our genetic nature to essentially steal the labor and life of others for our own advancement.

1.8 million years later, enter in 1960's feminism.

Feminism unto itself was not a bad thing, even in its viral 1960's form. Equal rights, women's suffrage, equal opportunity, etc., are all valid, noble, and legitimate aims. The problem was it served as a slippery-slope-catalyst by which to frame the sexes into an "us vs. them," a "men vs. women" adversarial relationship. This new paradigm was dangerous because it not only played well (if not, outright succumbed) to human nature's desire to live off of others, but it also gave women the excuse, the green light, and the rationale to be lazy, entitled, and self-pitying, and ultimately the authority to steal from others, specifically men. They were "victims." They were "oppressed." They were kept down by the "patriarchy." And they deserved recompense.

Again, this is a bold claim and certainly not all women are like this, but one need only look at how feminism has evolved from an idealistic movement into a money-grubbing, victim-whoring, non-stop-nagging profession. This industry or "profession" does not produce a single, tangible bit of good or service. It doesn't solve or remedy any problem. A single lemonade stand ran by the local neighborhood kids for an afternoon produces more value to society than all of the women's studies departments ever have combined. And I dare you to find any women's studies class, book, thesis, or seminar that does NOT have as its final conclusion the theft and transfer of other people's money. If anything, feminism today is merely a political group that constantly whines, complains and demands the money of others…so that they might continue to whine, complain, and demand the money of others...so that they might continue to...etcetera, etcetera.

Normally and in the past, post 60's feminism and feminists were identified as the professional, white-collar panhandlers they were. Saner heads saw them for the parasites they had become and dismissed them as such. The problem is along with codifying feminism into an adversarial relationship against men, they also codified it into a profession. And that profession metastasized into a well-oiled machine in the colleges and universities. Worse, this well-oiled machine invariably infected the public schools, ensuring feminist indoctrination was embedded into the minds of all school children from the age of five to 25. Now, all women (and men) are to some level steeped in feminism, victimhood ideology, and anti-male indoctrination. And this is where the real threat lies.

A Feminist Success

It is impossible to measure something as intangible as what percent of women consciously and actively hate men. It's impossible to measure how many women today think they are actually oppressed. And it's impossible to gauge what percent of women think they're victims. But it is not so much a statistical number that matters, as much as it is that feminists and the education system have convinced a critical mass of them.

Using the Muslim community as an example, the vast majority of Muslims are not radical terrorists, bent on the destruction of the planet. Most of them just want to go about their day, raise their families, practice their religion, and be left in peace. But a roughly estimated 8% of them are radicalized and most certainly do pose a threat to the US, as well as the rest of the world.

The same applies to women who've gone through the US education system in the past 50 years. Yes, the majority of women do not hate men. The majority of women very much probably like men and wish them to do well. But it is without a doubt a critical percentage of women (as well as some men) have been co-opted by anti-male feminism and are true believers in the cause. And though we don't know the specific numbers, we see evidence in society of feminism's success, which also serves as a proxy as to how far the insanity has spread.

<u>The Women's March on Washington</u>

For example the 'Women's March on Washington' in 2017. The main march itself at the nation's capitol attracted around 750,000 attendees, while nationwide the protests garnered around 4 million. This is roughly 2.8% of the female population, but double that to safely assume not all women who wanted to attend the rally could. That means roughly 5.6% women truly believe the feminist dogma that they are somehow victims or oppressed.

But the real issue is not that feminist indoctrination successfully convinced 1 in 20 American women that they are victims or suffering under an oppressive patriarchal regime. It's that they got 750,000 women to spend their own money and time, taking off of work, purchasing flights and hotels, to knit and wear pink pussy hats to protest a completely legitimate democratic election. And they got another 3.25 million to do the same in their closer-by towns. That's not only a waste of precious time and money, it's insane. These people quite literally concluded the best use of their time and money that day was to protest a LEGITIMATE election by wearing pink pussy hats.

The Wage Gap

Another example: women's choice of college degrees. This is a particularly interesting one, because since feminists and feminism are so thoroughly ensconced in the education industry, they heavily lobby women to choose degrees that are politically aligned with feminism. Unfortunately, these degrees are also largely worthless, as they provide the student with no employable or in-demand skills. Worse, they saddle women with an unpayable level of student loans which will remain a financial albatross around their necks for the rest of their lives.

But simply majoring in a worthless subject is not an indication of bigotry against men or that someone has drank the feminist cool aid. Truth be told, the majority of women, feminist or not, choose worthless subjects as their majors. It is their hypocritical response to the consequences of doing so that exposes how successful feminism has been in brainwashing them. Specifically, the wage gap.

Let us be very clear. There is no wage gap. There is an effort gap. Men major in engineering at a rate of 4 men to every woman. Men also choose degrees in the world of computers, IT, programming, and computer networking. Men also work in fields that are more dangerous and physically demanding, such as cops, linemen, welders, miners, and oil rig workers (would just love to see a Women's Studies professor switch jobs with an oil rig worker in January). Men work more, putting in more overtime and taking less vacation. And finally, a big contributor to the wage gap, is the fact that men do not give birth to children. Regrettably, giving birth to a child is somewhat of a time-consuming process, not to mention that whole "raising your children" thing tends to keep women at home and off the corporate ladder.

The solution to any sane person who GENUINELY wants to close the wage gap, who GENUINELY wants to see women be as successful as men, who GENUINELY CARES about women would be to tell women to stop majoring in "International Studies" and instead crack open a calculus book or learn to program Python. To stick around for extra hours at the office. And to take fewer sick leave and personal days. This would close the wage gap overnight and solve a problem that has plagued women for years.

However, women, and especially feminists, have a different theory and therefore a different solution: blame everything on men.

It's "sexism."
It's "male privilege."
It's "the glass ceiling."
It's "the good ole boys' network."

It's anything but their own foolish mistake to major in "International Transgender Communication Studies" or take seven "personal days" a week.

Worse, their proposed solution to the wage gap is the exact same thing they're protesting against – sexism. They demand special treatment and preferential hiring status over men. They euphemistically call this "affirmative action," but no matter what they call it, *it is genuine sexism* to favor one person over a better-qualified person because of their genitalia. Worse still, the world bends over backwards for these people, humors their delusion, and actually buys it. Affirmative action is not only the law of the land, but is a standard hiring policy of every major US employer, as well as every government department. In other words, IT IS STANDARD POLICY TO DISCRIMINATE AGAINST MEN.

Again, the issue is not so much the hypocrisy of affirmative action, women's poor choice in degrees, the abandonment of meritocracy, or how it is now official policy to discriminate against men. It's that such things are proof of how successful feminism has been in getting people to be unanchored from reality and morality.

Body Mutilation and "Fat Acceptance"

In the 60's and 70's, true believers in the feminist religion burned their bras. Perhaps a bit childish. Perhaps a bit sophomoric. But most of those women grew up, matured, returned to reality, and became productive members of society. Some became accountants. Some became secretaries. Most of them wed and had children. And most of them went on to lead normal lives.

The reason why is that deep down inside, no matter what feminist slop they were being fed, they were female. They were feminine. Like the billions of women before them over the millions of years in human history, they wanted to have a family and raise children. And they knew that in order to do that they would have to maintain a certain level of physical beauty to attract a man. Oh, sure, some of them may have protested they were not going to be any man's "plaything." Or that beauty was "on the inside." But if the volume and variety of women's beauty magazines, fashion shows, and movies told us anything, it's that deep down inside women knew men liked beauty, and they would spend trillions over the course of their lives getting it.

The problem is that to be beautiful is to suffer because being attractive, whether you're male or female, requires a lot of work. You need to work out, you need to diet, you need to dress right, and this says nothing about developing personality traits such as charm, humor, and being lovely. And while most women secretly acknowledge this (why else is dieting such a large industry) the time and effort required to be beautiful is so tremendous, it's just too daunting for many women to commit to.

This has resulted in quick fixes or compromises that are more popular among women than actually putting in the time and toil to become beautiful. Half-assed dieting programs. "Power walking." Clothes that purportedly make a bad body look good. Constantly changing hairstyles. And perhaps the quintessential example of this is the trend of using nails, heels, and weaves in the futile hope that men won't realize you are indeed fat. Anything and everything to avoid the life-long pain and agony of the treadmill and the gym that beauty demands.

But feminism offered a much easier alternative – to hell with the gym. More specifically, to hell with men. You don't need them. Beauty is defined by us, and it has no definition. We are all beautiful and nobody can tell us any different.

This was a very tempting proposition indeed. Once again playing to human's default nature to be lazy, simply giving up men would free women of a life-long chore of dieting, working out, and hitting the gym. They would also be freed of putting on makeup, wearing heels, or whatever other degrading hurdles men were requiring of them. Plus they wouldn't have to have any of that nasty, dirty, disgusting sex. A life free of labor, toil, and effort, liberating women to do what they truly wanted in life.

There was just one minor problem. Two million years of human evolution said otherwise.

No matter what lies you want to tell yourself, both men and women are hard wired to have some unremoveable preferences, tastes, desires, and instincts.

For example I like boobs.

Man, do I love boobs.

Ever since hitting puberty I have held a pro-boob political platform in my life. I want to see them, I want to play with them, they rank up there with ice cream and video games in terms of the joy and happiness they bring to my life. Matter of fact, even if I were to die a long, protracted Alzheimer's death, the last word I would sputter before my ultimate demise will be "booooooobsssss."

But I live in reality. I don't live in denial. I am forever programmed to love boobs and the female form (no matter how much pain that might cause me in the long run) and I accept this. But feminists and women who claim they don't want men don't. They are in denial. They are living a lie. And though it may seem an easier and preferable route to ignore reality by sticking your head in the sand, this puts reality and your beliefs on a collision course, which is guaranteed to cause you incredible damage when they collide. And this damage manifests itself today in the increasing trend we see of "body mutilation" and "fat acceptance."

By "body mutilation" I mean everything women do to mar their bodies.

Nose piercings.
Tongue piercings.
Tongue splittings.
Eyebrow piercings.
Nipple piercings.
Even genitalia piercings.

Shaved hair.
Short hair.
Blue hair.
Red hair.
Skrillex hair.
Or the ironic retaining of armpit hair.

And tattoos.

Mercy. The tattoos.

Tattoos with Chinese symbols.
Tattoos with the Namaste symbol.
Tattoos with stupid sayings.
Tattoos with misspelled words.
Tattoos that "express yourself."
Tattoos that "define yourself."
Tattoos on your cleavage.
Tattoos above your genitalia.
Tattoos on your ass.
The armband tattoo.
The barbed wire tattoo.
Trampstamps.
Sleeves.
Neck sleeves.
Leg sleeves.
Spine sleeves.
And let's not forget tear tattoos below your eyes.

All these things mar a woman's body and
lessens her beauty.

When it comes to "fat acceptance" I mean when
women reject men's preference for a slender, fit
body, and replace it with their own desire to be
obese and fat.

"Big is beautiful."
"Inner beauty."
"Beauty has no number."
"Health at any size."
"Women with curves."
"BBW."
"Fat shaming."
"You're shallow for not liking fat chicks."
And let's not forget that timeless old classic, "My friend has a great personality."

Like tattoos, ear gauges, and skrillex haircuts, fat mars a woman's body and lessens her beauty.

While on the face of it these two phenomena may seem to be proof that women are successfully rejecting men's demand that women be beautiful, it is quite the opposite. For if you truly didn't care what men thought you would quietly go your own way and do your own thing. You wouldn't hit the gym. You wouldn't hit the treadmill. You wouldn't apply makeup. You'd read books, you'd pursue your profession, you'd pursue your hobbies, you'd do whatever it is you wanted to do in your life. You are truly free. You wouldn't give a damn whether men thought big was disgusting or that a sleeve was revolting.

But they don't.

Like an ex-girlfriend who claims she hates you, but yet keeps contacting you, body mutilation and fat acceptance are proof positive women are still obsessed what men and society think about them. This is why "fat acceptance" isn't a quiet, monastic movement, but a loud, in-your-face one where women **DEMAND** society acknowledges "big is beautiful." This is why obese women, and women in general, are constantly telling each other how beautiful they are, when it is men, and not themselves, that ultimately determine if they're beautiful. And dare you critique a woman's mutilated mural of piercings, tattoos, ear gauges, and skrillex, be prepared for a violent screed about how you are a bigoted, sexist pig that doesn't know true beauty when you see it. Because deep down inside these women know they aren't beautiful and have used "fat pride" and body mutilation as a surrogate for purpose and meaning in life.

But if you thought that was insane, the real insanity begins when these women think shaming men, guilt-tripping men, and haranguing men is going to get them to find what is repulsive, beautiful and what is ugly, hot. That yelling and screaming at men will override millions of years of human evolution, genetic programming, and biological hardwiring, and then magically - "POOF" - we all want to date loud, obnoxious, fat, mutilated, tongue-pierced women. And may I point out the additional irony that it is tyrannical to deny men "the right to choose" what we deem to be beautiful or not?

Again, this is feminist-originated insanity defined. And again, the question is "how far has the feminist rot gone this time?" And again, the answer is "surprisingly far."

Not that every woman who has a tattoo is mentally damaged or lives vicariously through her tattoos, but 59% of American women have tattoos compared to 41% of men. From here the tattoo statistics become a little less consistent and reliable, but in general younger people are having more tattoos than older people and more women are walking into the tattoo parlor than men. The point is the overall trend is for more and younger women to have tattoos. Again, this doesn't mean if a woman has a tattoo she can't be the mother of your children. But while a discreet tattoo here or a Chinese proverb there isn't the mark of a delusional, man-hating feminist, a neck sleeve or arm sleeve that could be mistaken for a turtle-neck sweater is an aposematism. Do not make the mistake that being critical of women's tattoos is prudish or fuddy-duddyish. Like Mike Pence, being prudish and fuddy-duddy likely spared him the fate of Justice Kavanaugh.

When it comes to fat acceptance, feminism has made significant inroads into deluding society as well. Admittedly, some of this is just marketing as Oprah didn't become a billionaire telling women they were fat, and women have always complimented one another on how beautiful they are (regardless of any proof). But the mainstream is starting to celebrate obesity, if for no other reason than it's profitable. Target Corporation now proudly boasts overweight models. Increasingly large women are gracing the covers of various fashion magazines. Young boys wearing makeup are doing the same. And now transgendered men are on the cover of Playboy. This may get these companies the business of the now 62% of women who are obese, but it normalizes this behavior harming no one but women themselves.

The end result is an "Emperor Has No Clothes" nightmare where we have to lie about female beauty. Men cannot express their genetic preference for skinny, attractive women because it would be sexist. Men are shallow for being the way nature programmed them. Women don't need men, condemning themselves to a life of misery, loneliness, spinsterism and cats. While corporations, colleges, political parties, and media all profit off of selling women the lie that they're all beautiful. And dare any one of you men step out of line and point out the emperor has no clothes, why that's just proof you hate women, you are the enemy, women are victims, and something needs to be done about it.

A New Environment and Mindset

We could go on using tangential and indirect methods to measure and approximate just how far feminism has infected society.

The percent of women who view themselves as a "strong feminist" (17%).
Google trend searches for "Toxic Masculinity" or "male privilege,"

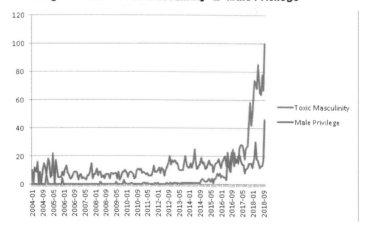

The percent of boys put on Ritalin vs. girls (didn't look it up).

The epidemic of "manspreading" (look it up).
Cite the nauseating number of news stories about "women's empowerment" and nothing about men.
Or delve into the world of education where boys are being raised to be girls (which would require its own book).

The larger point is feminism has been "successful enough" in convincing a critical percent of society of its propaganda. This doesn't mean turning people into man-haters, but it has co-opted enough people to at least believe the narrative that women are oppressed, they are victims, men and sexism (mindless or malicious) are to blame, and women have the right to be angry and demand justice in some form. They also have convinced enough American institutions (the media, Corporate America, the education system, and the Democrat Party) of this narrative giving credence and power to it. It is now perfectly legal to discriminate against men. It's perfectly fine to give women preferential treatment over men. You cannot speak bluntly or truthfully about the sexes. Women are constantly worshipped and praised, while somehow being continually convinced they're oppressed. And you're simply accused of sexism if you disagree. There has never been such a thorough and complete echo chamber designed around protecting and serving women, including shielding them from reality and responsibility, should any individual woman choose to live in it.

Unfortunately, this environment has also created the perfect conditions for a society-wide mentality to cement. The mentality feminists dreamed of where it is a "men vs. women," "us vs. them" world. Men and women no longer work together as they once did generations ago, but are divided along sexual lines, skeptical and distrusting of one another. This has cost us in terms of the joy the sexes once gave one another, destroyed the nuclear family, wreaked unfathomable mental stress on one another, and have turned us into scared, sterile robots to the point college students effectively need a signed legal contract to have sex in California. But when you throw in the narrative that men are the oppressors and women are the oppressed, and a critical number of women steeped in this new mentality believe it, some of those women are going to do more than merely protest or complain. They're going to go on the offensive. And it doesn't matter if you're guilty or not. They've been brainwashed enough to be thoroughly convinced you are. They were the victim, you were the enemy. They deserve justice, you deserve punishment. They will go on the warpath and there's nothing you can do to stop them.

"When Weaponized Women Attack"

A no name friend of mine, at a no name place was telling me the story of getting coffee and donuts for his office. It was Friday and his supervisor got stuck in traffic and was unable to get the obligatory Friday morning donuts. Upon getting into the office he told my friend "Here's some money. Get some donuts. Grab Suzie from marketing to see what kind of donuts they want."

So off my friend went to fetch Suzie. They hopped in his car. They got the donuts. And they returned to the office.

An hour later my buddy was called into his supervisor's office. Apparently, there was a complaint filed against him by Suzie. My buddy's heart dropped into his stomach. A wave of dread came over him. And before he could get angry at the preposterous claim he did something wrong, a paralyzing fear struck him as his mind raced through all the possible and horrific permutations of outcomes should he lose his job.

Before it got any worse, the boss calmed my friend's fears as he said there was nothing to be worried about. Suzie did not accuse my friend of doing anything, it's just that she felt "uncomfortable around him" and thought she should bring it to the attention of my friend's supervisors.

My friend sat there completely stunned.

That 45 minute event, that short, brief, bit of nothing, that mere unmentionable errand in a decade's long career, has now made my friend completely bigoted and apprehensive of working with young females. He now distrusts women under a certain age and I guarantee you, should he ever get into a position of power it will weigh negatively against women. And I can hardly blame him. He looked into the abyss. He got a peek into the other side. And like our Vice President, he is never being left alone with a woman at work ever again.

This unfortunate anecdote is unfortunately the "best" outcome should a feminist or weaponized woman decide to attack. My buddy was not reprimanded. My buddy was not disciplined. No real complaint was filed. Just a footnote that is now in his employment record that he made a precious snowflake "uncomfortable." The girl wasn't even malicious about it, as she was obviously conditioned by her education and society to "see something, say something." But that is what makes this story so scary - she didn't decide to "attack." This was merely procedure in her mind. Just "what you're supposed to do." She lacked the experience, foresight, and judgement to discern whether it was worth giving a man a heart attack just because she felt uncomfortable around someone. And she didn't realize how she inadvertently negatively affected the careers of future women. Suzie has since left the company and is now likely terrorizing the employees of another employer, but not without leaving her mark at my buddy's company.

Then there's the curious case of Joel Kaplan. Joel Kaplan was Facebook's Vice President of Global Public Policy. An otherwise stuffy title, but Joel caused more drama than a Telemundo soap opera when he was found attending the Kavanaugh hearings. Kaplan was a friend of the Kavanaugh family and was there to show his support.

This did not sit well with the weaponized women (and brainwashed men) of Facebook.

Completely ignoring an individual's right to hold differing political opinions, and believing they had a right to determine whether an employee in their company should participate in the political process - not a few, not a handful, not even a dozen - but HUNDREDS of Facebook employees took to the company's internal message board to complain about Kaplan's attendance.

Zuckerberg was forced to hold an emergency meeting where he both assuaged the irrational concerns of the little Hitlers he hired, while also defending Facebook's policy towards respecting its employees' right to participate in politics and hold differing opinions. However, perhaps in an attempt to feed the lions some meat, Cheryl Sandberg, Facebook's COO, still found it necessary to lecture Kaplan about the inappropriateness of his attendance given his high profile position at Facebook.

Like a coward, he apologized and said he should not have attended the hearings without permission from Daddy Mark and Mommy Cheryl. But his job was now most certainly jeopardized, and for what? Because he dared attend a hearing for a friend? Because he didn't believe a woman's 36 year old unproven claim? Because he didn't automatically and mindlessly "believe women?"

The fate of Mr. Kaplan is yet to be determined, but again look at how thoroughly indoctrinated and arrogant young women have become. You, as a private citizen, are not allowed to participate in politics feminists and weaponized women don't approve of. And even though you did nothing wrong, did nothing to them, and are participating in a personal matter in your personal life outside of work, they still deem it their right and authority to get you fired over it.

While Mr. Kaplan may or may not keep his job, this incident shows women are increasingly prone to complain about things at work, both legitimate and illegitimate. They also seem to lack the judgement to determine what is their business and what is none of their business at all. This is proven as sexual harassment complaints are on the rise. In part prompted by the #meetoo movement and the Harvey Weinstein saga, the EEOC reports a full 50% increase in sexual harassment complaints from 2016 to 2017. No doubt many of these complaints are legitimate, but given the "us vs. them" mentality thoroughly embedded in the minds of women, it raises the question how many innocent men are being falsely accused? If merely feeling "uncomfortable" around a man or a man "being a Republican" is enough for women to file a complaint, how many of these men are getting false-accusation-induced heart attacks at work? How many men (and their families) are having their livelihoods threatened because of wrong-think?   Are these legitimate complaints or is it a firestorm feeding off of itself and turning into a witch hunt?

Disgusting as it is that many of these weaponized women are veritable dictators, thinking their politics trump individuals' rights to political opinions - or worse, are so mindless and brainwashed that normal male behavior gets misconstrued as "making me feel uncomfortable" or "harassment" - these are still the best possible outcomes in that nobody had lost their jobs. My buddy is still employed. Mr. Kaplan is still employed. They merely had "career scares" and will henceforth dance lightly around the eggshells of easily offended women.

But what if you did get fired?

The story of Larry Summers is the perfect example of offending the increasingly fragile political feelings of feminists, leftists, weaponized women, and tyrants at work. During his tenure as the president of Harvard University he spoke at a conference about the "greater male variability" theory. This theory states that males have greater variability in nearly all aspects and functions compared to females. That the female population tends to more tightly congregate around an average, while men are more widely dispersed. This is both good and bad for men in that there are more men at both the "good" and "bad" ends of every spectrum. There are more men who are fatter and skinnier than women. There are more men with no musical ability and greater musical ability than women. And there are many more rich men than women, just as there are many more homeless men than bag ladies. Where Mr. Summers ran afoul of these professional victims was when he used this theory to explain why there were more men in the sciences and engineering.

This resulted in howls and cries of sexism from the usual victim-whoring suspects. Never mind that Dr. Summers was trying to explain an actual real-world phenomenon. Never mind Dr. Summers was attempting to explain this phenomenon with the goal of getting more women into the sciences. Never mind his goal was to help women and advance society. It was more important to the petulant little minds of the perpetually-offended that he hurt the fragile emotions of feminists. And that's when the weaponized women came out. The "Harvard Faculty of Arts and Sciences" board voted for his removal, ending his career and discrediting Harvard University as a legitimate institution of education.

Then sometimes getting fired is the best thing that can happened to you, as was the case with one Jian Ghomeshi.

Mr. Ghomeshi was a Canadian musician and radio show host for the Canadian Broadcasting Corporation. That was until he was accused of sexual harassment at work and summarily fired. And keep in mind by "harassment" his accuser meant:

"Emotional abuse, too: gaslighting and psychological games that undermined her intelligence, security and sense of self. Sometimes that hit harder than the physical trespassing."

Whether this constituted actual harassment was moot, because then three more women came forward to accuse him of sexual assault, including "choking and four counts of sexual assault." While losing his job was bad enough, Mr. Ghomeshi now faced a prison sentence and the fact his life was effectively over.

That was until the trial, where the testimony of his accusers was so bad, so contradictory, and so patently false, the judge dismissed the charges and Mr. Ghomeshi was acquitted.

The 20 seconds of dread my friend endured for making a girl feel "uncomfortable" was bad enough. I cannot possibly begin to fathom what it was like for Mr. Ghomeshi to endure years of dread not only losing his job, but facing the likelihood he would be put in a cage for a significant percent of his remaining life. I cannot imagine the rage and anger he felt for being falsely accused not of "harassment" or "annoying" somebody, but of an actual crime and a sexual one no less. And even though he's been exonerated, even though he has moved on, how do you pick up the pieces and move on from that? Going forward I'm sure Mr. Ghomeshi is going to "believe women" and I'm sure he's not going to let this personal hellish experience negatively affect his future interactions with women.

If you don't think it can get any worse, it most certainly can because while sexual harassment is bad, and sexual assault is worse, actual rape is unforgivable. And the only thing arguably worse is being falsely accused of it.

You would think something as serious as rape would be a no-go zone. That nobody is that depraved, that vile, that evil that they would falsely accuse a man of rape. That no matter how bad the relationship between men and women deteriorates in this country, no woman would stoop so low so as to falsely accuse a man of rape. Well think again, because a short quick visit to today's American college campuses will show you NOT a "rape culture" (as feminists and women contend), but a "fake rape accusation culture" where women are outright lying about one of the most disgusting atrocities a human can commit.

There's the Duke lacrosse team scandal where a stripper and prostitute by the name of Crystal Gail Magnum accused three Duke lacrosse players of gang rapping her. There was the additional tinge of racism as Ms. Magnum was African American and the accused were white, introducing the salaciousness of a hate crime. Without an investigation, without proof, and without any evidence, the world seemingly "believed women" and judged these men guilty of the crime. The lacrosse season was canceled, the LaCrosse coach unfairly fired, and the case was prosecuted by a zealous, petty, power-tripping weaponized man, Mike Nifong.

Though the prosecution and pitch-fork carrying mob of public opinion came in strong, Ms. Magnum's testimony started to change as well as contradict itself. The North Carolina bar filed ethics charges against Nifong including dishonesty, fraud, deceit and misrepresentation. Nifong was also found criminally guilty of lying for which he served jail time. And in the end it turned out Ms. Magnum had been lying all along, perhaps for attention, perhaps because of racial reason, perhaps because of mental reasons, perhaps because she was intoxicated, the reasons are a bit unclear. Regardless, the case was dropped, but not without first ruining the lives of the three men falsely accused of rape. Ms. Magnum did not serve any jail time for ruining these men's lives, but she was sentenced to prison for second degree murder in 2013 on a completely separate case.

Then there's the *Rolling Stone* Magazine false rape accusation scandal. Here it isn't clear who the true villain is. Jackie Coakley who made up the accusation to win the affection of a boy she liked or (as she later recanted) "she believed it at the time?" Or Sabrina Rubin Erdely who wrote the bogus *Rolling Stone* piece in the first place? Regardless, the article claimed that Ms. Coakley had been gang raped at the Phi Kappa Psi fraternity at the University of Virginia as part of a fraternity initiation ritual. The police conducted an investigation which quickly pointed towards the story and the accusation being false. But not without the University of Virginia suspending the fraternity and a nation-wide hate-fest directed at fraternities in general.

In the end the fraternity may have been exonerated, but not without several lawsuits being filed. The University of Virginia sued Rolling Stone Magazine and Ms. Erdely for $3 million. Phi Kappa Psi sued Rolling Stone for $25 million. A tertiary law suit has been filed and approved. But oddly enough Ms. Coakley, the one who started it all, was neither the target of a lawsuit or criminal charges.

Lauren Emily Pearson was not so lucky. After falsely accusing one Cesar Antonio Lopez of raping her at a college dorm party, once her story started to fall apart, the police arrested her instead. This is of course only after Mr. Lopez was arrested, spent several nights in jail, burdened family and friends with coming up with bail money, and got kicked out of college. But at least Ms. Pearson was arrested for filing a false police report…even though no charges were pressed.

And if you're hoping for a little bit of justice, there's the story of Nikki Yovino where this same fake campus rape accusation fad continues its tiring refrain. This time the then 18 year old Nikki made a fake rape accusation against two college football players at Sacred Heart University. Her reason was valid enough – she wanted to garner sympathy from another boy she was interested in and thought accusing men of rape would get her that attention. Never mind the short-sightedness of this incomprehensibly stupid plan. Never mind the horrific damage she would cause the falsely accused. She wanted to get a boy and her prospective romantic dalliances were more important than the livelihoods of those two poor football players. Sadly, both football players lost their scholarships; neither of them getting them back, and both dropped out of school. But the good news is a judge actually decided to punish a weaponized woman for lying about rape. Ms. Yovino was sentenced in the summer of 2018 to a whole, single year in prison.

We could go on, but the number of fake rape accusations (on college campuses or not) is nearly limitless. Any internet search will show you just how pervasive and successful feminism has been in getting weaponized women to resort to this disgusting tactic. Thankfully, we have a judicial system to ensure only the guilty are sent to jail. And when there's a false rape accusation saner heads prevail. Police investigations prove guilty men innocent, and though those men's lives are ruined in the process, they can move on in their lives as they've at least avoided prison.

Or have they?

Because if you think getting kicked out of school, getting fired, losing your scholarship, having your reputation ruined, and looking at 10 to 20 years in prison all because of a false rape accusation was bad, what if you were actually convicted of a rape you didn't commit?

This was the case of Gregory Counts and VanDyke Perry.

Both Counts and Perry were accused and convicted of rape in 1991. Their accuser (who is oddly never named in any of the articles written about them) claimed Counts, Perry and a third man gang-raped her in Central park. The prosecution's evidence was shoddy, the accuser's testimony contradictory, and the police investigative work unprofessional, leading to their erroneous convictions. The entire judicial system failed these two men, resulting in Perry losing 10 years of his life to prison and Counts an unforgivable 26. Thankfully, they were exonerated in 2018.

The horrors suffered and the price paid by men merely falsely *accused* of rape is already unimaginable. But there are no words in the English language to describe what it's like to be wrongly convicted of a crime you didn't commit and to lose your entire youth to prison. And though there's a very small statistical chance you might get wrongly convicted of rape, the case of Counts and Perry should make the compelling argument that *you shouldn't even let it get to the point where you're potentially facing a judge under a false accusation*.

If there's anything you should learn from

1. The Kavanaugh-Ford debacle
2. The hysteria of false rape on college campuses
3. The "us vs. them" mentality successfully installed by feminism
4. The overall anti-male environment of the country
5. The increasing number of weaponized women, and
6. The Counts and Perry convictions

it's that you need to take proactive, pre-emptive, and preventative measures against this threat. Understand that though the majority of women appreciate men, there are enough women out there who hate them. There are enough women who are believe they are the victim. There are enough women who believe you are the oppressor. There are enough women who are on the perpetual hunt to be offended and victimized. And there are enough women who are fully prepared to lie about it. And whether it's to protect their reputation, advance a political agenda, get revenge, attract a man, or simply be an attention-whore some of them won't even think twice about ruining your career, ruining your life, ruining your family, ruining your reputation, or throwing you in jail. You need to realize this because it is true.

Why Do They Attack?

The burning question is why do some women do this? What leads a woman to destroy a man's career? What leads a woman to falsely accuse men of rape? What leads a woman to take a petty and minor inconvenience, perhaps no sin at all, and spin it into a yarn of a full blown sexual harassment case? The answer is complex but can be found in the primordial political morass detailed in the "Origins" section of this handbook.

Revisiting "Origins," it is in the biological nature of every human to at least be tempted by laziness as a path towards survival and advancement. This makes some sense as conserving energy was vital to survival in the past. But if you put morality aside, you could be really lazy and steal somebody's labor, food, women, cattle, etcetera, and drastically improve your chances for survival. This temptation to steal is always there and it is morality (or at least) *the law* that prevents most people from doing so today.

But with the introduction of feminism in the 1960's, women in particular were given a narrative that could excuse them from stealing or benefiting at the expense of men. That narrative was they were oppressed, they were victims, and they were entitled to favorable treatment in the laws, hiring practices, educational opportunities, etcetera, in order to put them on par with men. The trick to getting this narrative to stick was that you had to villainize and criminalize men and male behavior. You had to take a system that had been in balance for millions of years, and claim it was flawed, claim it was wrong, and needed to be fixed. Therefore, staying at home, raising children, and maintaining that home was not loving work you did for your family. It was oppression. And men majoring in engineering, getting shot in wars, working in coal mines, spending 10 years in med school, and therefore making more than female school teachers was not hard work or economics. It was sexism. And running around, getting in fights, chasing girls, pulling their hair, bringing snakes into the classroom, and catcalling women was not normal male behavior. It was "toxic masculinity." A clear line had to be drawn that designated male as being bad and female as being good. And any disparity between the sexes was reason to call for income transfers, government programs, financial aid, hiring preferences, bogus lawsuits, and a whole host of other lazy benefits women enjoy over men today, should they choose to.

Again, it bears repeating, the majority of women are NOT maliciously or consciously participating in this racket. Many women in fact hate this racket and either genuinely support themselves through hard work and labor, or stay at home to lovingly raise their family, or a combination of both. But there is a critical mass of women who use the excuse to be lazy that feminism has given them, and these are the women this handbook is trying to warn you about.

The problem, though, is that in order to understand why "weaponized women attack" you can't just say "laziness" or "feminism" because at most that is tangentially the case. Feminism merely provides the ideology or religion from which other excuses are derived. But when you delve a little further, researching and reading all the court cases and news stories, there is a rhyme and reason, there is a logic, and specific reasons for women's false accusations start to form. There is, of course, no official list, but based on my research roughly eight reasons exist. Some of them overlap one another, others are completely independent on their own, but whatever the case they share a similar kernel in victimhood ideology and feminism.

"The True Believer"

The true believer is the least malicious, and at times, the completely innocent one. She truly doesn't know any better and is merely a product of her education, indoctrination, and parenting...or lack thereof. She doesn't mean any ill-will towards men, but has been brought up in an environment where it is just assumed men are harassers, men do bad things, and "according to my Women's Studies 101 class, I'm supposed to report them." This was the case with "Suzie" who mindlessly reported she was "uncomfortable" around my buddy.

"Mental Disorder"

Also somewhat benign are women with mental disorders. This is a bit more difficult to diagnose because you don't know if a woman is accusing you of something because she's insane or because she's swallowed the cool aid. Unfortunately, you don't even know if the girl has an actual mental disorder or claims she does because it's trendy or popular to have one nowadays.

Ultimately, it doesn't matter if she does because she's making the accusation just the same. But you will definitely want to steer clear of women who either have, or claim to have, bi-polar disorder. An acquaintance of mine was living with a feminist who was also bi-polar. It was so bad that he knew if he told her he was moving out, she would bash her wrists on countertops, bruise herself, and then make a false battery accusation. He had the foresight to have a cop chaperone him when he told her he was moving out and proceeded to immediately do so. The look on her face I hear could melt granite.

"Attention Whores"

From here on out the list only includes evil people. There is some understanding if you're completely brainwashed and were never introduced to a different opinion in your entire educational career. It's also understandable if you have a genuine mental illness. But falsely accusing two men of rape, as Nikki Yovino did, is vile and evil.

Unfortunately, this is more common than one would like to admit, especially if the girls are younger. They think some kind of drama, some kind of crisis will catch the attention of a boy they like, or perhaps make them popular at school. Regardless of their flawed reason, they are so self-centered, so self-important, they value social status and attention more than they do the lives of the innocent men they accuse. And while these women will not be carrying signs that say "I'm an attention whore," be on the look-out for any women who seem to act like one.

"Revenge"

Perhaps the opposite of being an attention whore is revenge. Usually this is the result of a guy rejecting the interest of a girl or breaking up with a girl he no longer wishes to date. And if you don't know what the saying, "Hell hath no fury like a woman scorned" means, look it up so you don't learn through experience. I personally have had my tires slashed, car keyed, even been stalked because I dared to decide I no longer wanted to spend my time with certain women. But stalking and slashed tires are HIGHLY PREFERABLE outcomes to being falsely accused of rape, battery, or assault as a target of revenge. I strongly recommend you do the same as my colleague and maybe hire a police chaperone if you're debating dumping your Gender Studies girlfriend, who's on anti-depressants, and reads Sylvia Plath.

"Justice or Fanaticism"

Unlike revenge, which is usually for personal reasons, 'justice' is for political reasons as is used in the sense of "social justice warrior." These women are not only true believers in feminism, but they REALLY do view you as the enemy. And not only do they view you as the enemy, they have it in their minds that you have benefited unfairly and owe them some sort of reparations.

Sadly these fanatics, like all fanatics have nothing else going on in their lives, and therefore only have their religion or cult to draw value from. And since they have absolutely nothing else in life, this makes them feral and mental. Do not think for a second that if you cross them they won't slap a fake harassment suit on you or claim you created a "hostile work environment," all in an attempt to get you fired from your job or kicked out of school. These people live to be offended, they live to be victims, they eat, breathe, and sleep victim politics. You can often find them closing down highways when they don't get their way in life.

"Politics"

Somewhat overlapping fanatics are women who put their politics first and foremost in their lives.

They aren't necessarily as fanatical about their politics, as much as they are loyal. This loyalty is nearly unbreakable because not only is politics all they have in life, they lack the work ethic to go forth and invest in something else, forcing them to constantly recommit and double down on something that is ultimately pointless and unrewarding. This only reinforces their loyalty to their politics and they remain wedded to the cause until they die. These women tend to be older and will gladly sacrifice themselves for the party. Christine Blasey Ford is the poster child of this group of women, but they could also be stereotyped as career politicians (Hillary Clinton for example) or nearly every Women's Studies professor.

"Power Trippers"

Unlike the rest of the categories, this group has no anchoring in feminism or lazy politics. It's just pure human genetics. Sometimes it feels good to smite somebody and sometimes women go on a power trip just because they can. This is arguably the most dangerous group in that it's completely unpredictable. If you ever goof up, say something awkward, and find yourself at the mercy of a woman, she may just smite you for kicks.

"Hatred"

This is the simplest, but most evil reason some weaponized women attack. They just plain hate men. It could be they had a bad experience with their father. It could be they had a horrible ex. It could be they believe all the bad things feminism tells them about men. Or it could be some irrational bigotry. It just doesn't matter, they hate you.

To truly hate somebody because of a physical characteristic requires you be mentally ill. And thankfully, this is the minority of women. But that doesn't mean they're not out there or that their numbers aren't increasing. There was Christine Fair, the Georgetown professor who called for the castration of any white men in the senate who voted for Kavanaugh. There was Suzanna Danuta Walters, also a professor, who penned a piece called "Why Can't We Hate Men." There was "SCUM" (the Society for Cutting Up Men), a manifesto penned by a delusional woman named Valarie Solanas, that is somewhat macabrely celebrated among men haters today. And any internet search will find you thousands of more instances of women who hate men.

Thankfully, these women are the statistical rejects you're going to find when you have a population of 160 million women. But what is concerning, and should be of particular note to you, is the increasing numbers of women in the education system that hate men. It is not coincidental that both Ms. Fair and Ms. Walters come from the university system. And as pointed out before, feminism is ensconced in the education system, allowing them to project their bile and hatred into the young minds of nearly every child and adult in the country. Do not be surprised if the majority of false accusations are made by women either directly employed by the education industry or whose worldview was heavily skewed by it.

The Insanity Will Not Stop

We could delve further into these eight theoretical reasons if we wanted, but it's ultimately pointless why women attack. The only thing that matters is they do. But I wanted to highlight this list and try to address the reasons why weaponized women attack because it shows you something very important and very scary. Barring mental disorders, personal revenge, or power tripping, these reasons are all ideologically driven. They're all religions. And unless there's an explicitly stated goal or objective to be met by these religions, these women will never be satisfied.

For example take each reason and follow it to its logical end. What would it take to satisfy these women?

"True Believers" have swallowed feminism whole to the point it's part of their ethical and principled core. They will live their entire lives in the "us vs. them" dichotomy no matter how much evidence you try to introduce otherwise. One could even argue it's now part of their genetic hardwiring, bordering on instinct, and simply can't be removed from their psyches. So even if women reached parity with men, even if they surpassed men, these women would still operate from the erroneous premise it's "men vs. women," "us vs. them," "victim vs. the oppressor." You will not stop them.

"Attention Whores" put themselves first and foremost above all else. They're so addicted to attention or popularity, nothing will convince them to be sympathetic and altruistic, considering and respecting the moral rights of others. Bar psychological help or a grand epiphany, these people will live the rest of their lives always putting themselves ahead of others and society. You will not stop them.

The "Fanatics" who desire justice are also impossible to satisfy. No matter how much you try to reason with them or appease them it will never be enough because their entire value in life is based on them being oppressed. If they ever got the justice or restitution they sought, they would immediately find something else to complain about or be victimized over because that is what they live for. Not the justice, but the position of the eternal underdog who has to constantly fight for it. It gives them virtue, it gives them value, all without having to work a real job. You will not stop them.

When it comes to "Politics" feminism is merely (if you'll forgive the crassness) "socialism with tits." And socialism's natural end is the elimination of private property and total ownership by the state. Women who are wedded to the Democrat Party (or Labor Party, or Socialist Party depending on where you are) will not stop complaining until there's a tax rate of 100%, the government owns everything, you own nothing, everybody makes the same, and *even then* they'd still find something to complain about. And if you don't believe it, simply ask any democrat (male or female) "how much is enough" and they will not be able to answer because deep down inside the truth is "all." So until the Soviet Socialist States of America becomes a reality, these women will not relent. You will not stop them.

Finally, the "Haters." The logical end to this philosophy would simply be either the elimination or total enslavement of men. Certainly some of you may object to that, but you are not going to convince genuine misandrists otherwise. They are always going to hate men, whether you're all eliminated or not. You will not stop them.

The larger point is that these weaponized women will never stop. They will never go away. They will never relent. They are like The Borg. They will constantly hound, complain, whine, and howl about how unfair life is, how sexist men are, and how they're entitled to X,Y, and Z. And even if you give them everything they ask for, they will still continue to complain about *something* because that is what's at their core. And if you don't believe this or think this is overly rash, just look at how far they've gone in terms of overreach and outright insanity in society. And look at how they find increasingly and incredibly petty things as "proof" of oppression, sexism, and sexual harassment.

There's the handful of women who've accused President George H. W. Bush of telling a dirty joke and then pinching them in the ass. Admittedly that is unacceptable behavior, but the man is 93 years old, in a wheel chair, and likely isn't about his mental faculties. Still, this made headline news and is cited as some kind of proof of widespread harassment.

There's the website "makethemscared.com" that allowed people to anonymously accuse men of rape and name them online. I'm all for catching, stopping and (honestly) killing rapists. But I'm also against websites that allow people to slander, make false accusations against, and defame innocent people. This website had no verification, no fact checking, people could just randomly list "Joe Blow" as a rapist whether he was one or not. Since then a lawyer got ahold of them, and now you can no longer anonymously accuse people of rape, but if a guy stood you up, dumped you, or said something online you didn't agree with politically, you can now go to that site and list him as a rapist to the public.

There's the logically-wrong "believe women" movement. It's logically wrong because it's patently against logic. It doesn't make sense. It contradicts reality. You're supposed to just "believe" someone because they're a woman? As if women are not capable of lying? Anybody with a brain stem can figure out why this is wrong. But that didn't seem to stop this bit of insanity from infecting half the population when it came to Blasey Ford's 36-year-old-accusation. Feminism successfully planted in the minds of half the population that it is sexist to not believe a woman.

Related to that, the statute of limitations.

How far back are feminists, Democrats, and weaponized women going to go to get some dirt? Apparently, the answer is 36 years. They're going to go back to your high school years to see if they can get dirt on you. And that's just today. In the future they will be going back to junior high, then middle school, and soon if they found out you pulled Suzie Q's pony tail in the 3rd grade you will be brought up on sexual harassment charges when you run for city council 40 years later.

Of course, why wait for tomorrow when you can charge six year old boys with sexual harassment today? Sadly, there's more than one instance where a boy under nine has been charged or accused by their school of sexual harassment. There's Hunter Yelton who kissed a girl on the hand when he was six (https://www.washingtontimes.com/news/2013/dec/10/6-year-old-boy-suspended-sexual-harassment-over-ki/). There was an anonymous nine year old boy who was threatened with sexual harassment charges in Florida for writing a love note (http://www.nydailynews.com/news/national/boy-

9-face-sexual-harassment-charges-love-note-article-1.2432300). And there's another nine year old boy who was accused of sexual harassment for calling his teacher "cute." (https://www.foxnews.com/us/boy-9-suspended-from-school-for-sexual-harassment-after-calling-teacher-cute). Sadly, an internet search will turn up many more instances of "seven year old sexual predators."

This is particularly ominous in that it shows another overreach of power - a constant expansion of what is considered criminal or wrong by feminists and weaponized women. In the olden days you could ask a girl out at work, heck a lot of people ended up married that way! Now you get dragged in front of HR and are asked to leave. If you saw a pretty girl walking past your construction site, you could wolf-whistle or cat-call. Now that will get you an $800 fine in France. Passing a note in the 2nd grade will land you in the principal's office. Booze is the reason half of you are alive today, but now a girl can't give consent if she had any. And apparently all that booze I drank in college, the boobs I copped as a result, and that ice chunk I threw at a party in 1987 prevents me from certain federal positions.

But perhaps the true sign of how far these women are willing to take it; consider the lengths that would have been required to satisfy them over the Brett Kavanaugh nomination. You would effectively have to be Jesus Christ, truly sinless to pass their impossible-to-meet standards. You literally could not have drank in college. You literally could not have tried to press a girl for sex. You couldn't have screwed up at all. You couldn't even have had an obscure note written in your year book. They literally wanted a flawless, sinless man, which simply doesn't exist. This only exposed their true ulterior political motive and why they dragged that poor man through the hell they did.

But here is where it gets truly insane.

You could be Jesus Christ himself and they still would have attacked you. (If you were Bill Clinton, you would have "gotten off" scot-free). But if you were Jesus Christ, they would have attacked you. And the reason is simple.

They can simply lie.

Because even if you are flawless, even if you are a boy scout, even if you are the "Son of God" himself, if you go against their political goals, their fanatical ideology, their fake religion that gives their pointless lives value, or you are somebody they plain don't like, they'll simply make up something about you and lie. And I contend that's precisely what Christine Blasey Ford and the Democrats did.

Only a fool would believe that a woman who comes out of nowhere with a spurious accusation from 36 years ago, that cannot be proven, that cannot be corroborated, conveniently 48 hours before a man is about to be confirmed to the Supreme Court, is telling the truth. And the only other people who claim to believe that, don't, because they damn well know it was a lie created to advance a political agenda.

Therefore, the Ford-Kavanaugh debacle should serve as the ultimate warning to all men out there as to just how far some of these weaponized women will go. You could do everything right. You could live your life as clean and moral as possible. You could do everything under the sun to make yourself impervious to them, but they can simply lie and put you through a world of hurt. And if you're lucky you come out like Kavanaugh or Ghomeshi. If you're not, you come out like Counts and Perry.

I recommend neither in that you bulletproof yourself against the weaponized woman.

CHAPTER 3
HOW TO DEFEND YOURSELF

The actual Pence Principle followed by our Vice President is very simple.
:
Do not be alone with another woman without your wife.
And do not attend a party where alcohol is being served without your wife.

Though it may be simple it is highly effective. Vice President Pence doesn't have to worry about any false rape or sexual harassment accusations. He always has a witness should there be a weaponized woman nearby. And usually that witness is his wife, who is the only woman who matters to him. The rest of the world's women could have whatever opinion they want about Mr. Pence. He doesn't care as long as Mrs. Pence loves him.

While it works for our Vice President, there are a couple flaws in the original Pence Principle in that it doesn't easily or equally transfer over to every man in America. For example it presupposes you're married and have a readily available wife to witness that, yes, you did not touch that woman over there. This won't be of much help for younger or otherwise unmarried men. Also, the Pence Principle wouldn't have protected Mr. Pence had he been accused by Mrs. Ford. The Vice President did not get married till he was 25 and as the Democrats and weaponized women have shown us, they are fully prepared to go back to the age of 17 to make accusations. Another problem is the Vice President is…well…"older." The original Pence Principle works great for somebody who remembers Richard Nixon, whose generation may adhere to some remnants of traditional standards and ethics. But not for somebody who doesn't remember 9-11, whose classmates were accused of sexual harassment in the 2nd grade, and whose generation is trained to be constantly offended.

Because of this the principle has to be expanded and tailored beyond its original form so it addresses the majority of instances men can and will face in the future, and be of benefit to all men. This new and improved version of The Pence Principle will not be a silver bullet that guarantees against every and all fake accusations or attacks, but one that will greatly enhance the protection of all men both now and into the future. And while lessons can be extrapolated from the overall theory to apply to each individual's situation, there are just shy of a dozen major rules or "sub-principles" that constitute this new and expanded Pence Principle.

"Rape is Bad. Mmmmmkay?"

To see how out of touch most feminists and some political leftists are, a common refrain they use is that we need to "teach men not to rape." This is very telling because it shows you they have completely misdiagnosed the problem and are therefore condemned to fail at stopping it.

Every man knows rape is bad.
Every man knows not to rape.
But there's a statistical minority of them who don't care and are going to rape anyway.
Simply telling them "rape is bad" is not going to stop them.
And the reason why is they are evil, mentally ill, or both.

The unfortunate reason advocates of the "teach men not to rape" mantra pursue this futile strategy is because they want to believe in their minds it's possible to have a world without rape. It's possible to have a world without any problems. And instead of more practically hunting down rapists and killing them (which would serve as a much better deterrent than simply telling them not to) they think that by just lecturing and hounding all men they're going to get the 6% of committed psycho rapists not to. It's naïve, it's stupid, it's short sighted, it does nothing to lessen the chances of a woman getting raped, and it's insulting to men who hate and detest rape.

So I must apologize when I say the first and obvious part of the expanded Pence Principle is not to rape. And not only "not rape," but do not sexually assault any woman, do not sexually harass any woman, don't even bother them. The main and simple reason is to be innocent. To make sure you did not actually commit the crime or the offense you're accused of. In addition there's the whole moral argument why you shouldn't do these things in the first place, but if you're going to get accused of some kind of harassment or assault it's to your benefit to simply not have done it. Not only will this give you the moral high ground and confidence you did nothing wrong, but not committing the offense will also ensure there is no evidence that you did such a thing. And upon investigation the lack of evidence (or proof of evidence) will likely show you did nothing wrong and therefore exonerate you.

The real risk, however, is not that you might accidentally rape or assault someone. It's that the definition of these things is constantly changing and expanding. Admittedly, you're a man and admittedly, you're going to want women. And not all of us will be a charming George Clooney, let alone a sober one, or one a woman will want in the first place. It is almost a guarantee you are going to annoy and harass a woman over the course of your life. But try your best to keep it at a minimum. Again, the real risk here is not that any of you are actually going to go and rape a girl or sexually assault her. The real risk is that she is going to interpret what you do as harassment or even assault. And since the standard of this is always being lowered and diluted, don't even bother risking it and opt instead to say nothing and shut up.

Choose Your Women Carefully

Women do not like being painted with a "wide brush." They will always point out the exception to the rule. Their pretty friend who is an engineer. That one woman she knows who makes more money than her boyfriend. Her aunt who is a traditional housewife and Republican.

Good for them.

The problem is with what's at risk here, you need to approach women more like an actuary or a statistician in order to lower your risk of being falsely accused of some such thing. You can't afford to

lose your family,
lose your career,
lose your job,
get kicked out of school,
lose your kids,
lose your reputation,
lose your wife,
get kicked out of your profession,
and in essence, lose your entire life

all so you could prove how open-minded and understanding you were one time in college.

This doesn't mean a girl who's volunteering at the local women's shelter is some raging, anti-male feminist, but the following groups of women are red flags and pose a higher risk of ruining your life.

Women with Leftist Politics

Be they a feminist, a socialist, a communist, a liberal, a leftist, or just a run of the mill democrat, women with leftist politics are the highest risk group. The reason is simple – this is where this philosophy of anti-male sentiment, victimhood politics, feminism, and weaponized women originate from. At its core is the human genetic predisposition to be lazy, with feminism giving them the rationale to view men as the enemy and profit off of them. And whether they actually believe it or not doesn't matter because if they do they're a "true believer" and if they don't, then they're an opportunist and professional victim. Both are indoctrinated and prone to make fake accusations, view innocent social faux pas on the part of men as harassment, or outright lie out of ideological fanaticism. And most put their politics above everything else in life, placing more value on these variants of socialism than justice, fairness, innocence, love, friendship, happiness, and reality. This is the lions' den. Do not fish from this pool.

To what extent leftist politics and feminism have infected women today depends on a few factors. The majority of women are democrats, but that is due more to their caring and nurturing nature. These "normal democrats" are not vile, hate-filled feminists who wake up every day angry at men, finding new and creative ways as to find out how everything is men's fault. They're simply kind, caring women who want to help out society. But for every normal female democrat out there, there is one, likely two, probably three weaponized feminists. This heavily depends on age as a 70 year old grandmother of 10 is likely to be a caring democrat, while her 21 year old grand-daughter majoring in Political Science is likely to be a man-hating feminist raising awareness and empowering herself to start conversations.

The way to tell is very simple; see if they love people more than the government. If they love their fellow man more than their politics. If politics comes first in their life, or if life comes first over politics. For example, several years ago a younger girl I was dating was indeed a democrat. But she didn't mention it until we had been dating a full six months, almost in passing. She did however mention (many times) that she wanted children and to be a stay at home mom, maybe work as a florist part time. Here it was obvious she was a "good democrat" that loves people and life, has a soul, and has something more important than politics going on in her life. Contrast that with another woman I briefly dated. All this woman did was talk about her politics. She was a "feminist," she "voted for Hillary Clinton," she was working on "this political cause or that political crusade," and she had to get her masters in some worthless humanities degree or another (the major escapes me now). The point is if they tell you they're a feminist, they tell you they're a liberal, they have a bumper sticker on their car, or they wear it proudly on their shoulder, there is no reason to interact with such women on any level, be it dating, socializing, or working. They are not capable of long term, productive human interaction because they love their politics more than they do any human, and certainly more than any man.

Finally, if you're not too sure about cutting a swath as wide as eliminating left-leaning women from your life, look at the politics of the majority of false accusers and weaponized women. Yes, statistically speaking since the majority of women are democrats or leftists, the majority of false accusers will be the same. But here you must differentiate between the weaponized woman and a simple, caring democrat. Mrs. Ford, Prof. Fair, and Prof. Walters are all weaponized women in the sense they participate in radical leftist and feminist politics, hail from the university system, and put their politics above all else in life. The sweet, aspiring stay at home mother who happens to vote democrat does not, and is likely not going to falsely accuse you of some sexual crime.

Aposematisms

Closely related to leftist and feminist women, are women who are aposematisms. If you don't know what this means, an "aposematism" is a phenomenon in the animal kingdom where animals have bright colors and patterns that serves as a warning to any would-be-predators that they're poisonous. Predators see the bright colors and choose instead to find a non-poisonous meal.

Some women, thankfully, do you this favor; we covered them in the "Body Mutilation and Fat Acceptance" segment of this handbook. Quite literally weaponized women will dye their hair bright colors, shave half their head, pierce abnormal body parts, visibly tattoo large parts of their bodies, become morbidly obese, and will even deter men further with loud and obnoxious behavior (search "Trigglypuff"). Their behavior is so aberrant and they are so visually repulsive you won't want to have anything to do with them. It doesn't need to be stated to avoid these women in any and every endeavor.

The Stereotypical Rachel Maddow Look

You may laugh, and this axiom may go away if fashion trends change, but this rule is also highly effective and efficient because it works. If you see a woman who looks like Rachel Maddow, chances are she is a weaponized woman and you want nothing to do with her.

Like an aposematism, these women tend to have short hair, dress like men, wear no makeup, and seem addicted to wearing those damn thick rimmed glasses. The overall result is a woman who rejects femininity, female beauty, looks like a guy, all of which a barely-trained, half-blind eye can easily and visually identify. Worse, any woman sporting the Rachel Maddow look not only puts her politics and feminism first, but is also likely not terribly intelligent in that she's a conformist. Just like all the hipsters who wear salmon colored jeans and sport the same effeminate beards ironically and contradictorily disprove how independent minded they are, it's the same level of low-intelligence conformity with the Rachel Maddow look. Look for women who look like women.

Medicated Women

In 2010 a study was released that showed one in four women were on some form of mental health medication. The easy joke was that "3 in 4 were going untreated!" Funny and dark as that is, the large and increasing percent of women using mental health meds to treat anxiety, depression, AHDH and so forth is no joke. Not only because you wouldn't want women to suffer from these mental conditions, but worse, it's more likely women are increasingly using these drugs to cope with everyday life instead of an actual mental illness.

Whether it's an actual mental illness or they're using mental illness and drugs as a crutch, this is a higher risk group of women than those who do not use or abuse prescription drugs. Either because they have an actual mental illness or they're faking it which is worse. Again, there no doubt are women who are legitimately depressed and legitimately taking Adderall, but mental prescription drugs are a red flag. You have every right to rummage through your date's medicine cabinet looking for lithium. And you have every right to be wary of interacting with women who are on some kind of mental medication. There is no guarantee they will accuse you of sexual assault, but with the emotional side effects of these mind-altering drugs, why take the chance? Limit your exposure to these women to what is only necessary.

Academics, Humanities, and Liberal Arts Majors

Feminism, once again, lives in the world of college and Academia. It can't survive elsewhere because the real world demands profit, production, and something of value. Still, because feminism occupies this chokepoint of American society, it disproportionately influences society because nearly everybody must go through the education system at one point in their lives.

The level at which feminism is successful in indoctrinating students varies depending on the type of major a student chooses. Engineering majors, Accounting majors, and Pre-Med majors may be forced to take some pre-requisite classes in diversity or women's studies. Or they be forced into some kind of freshman orientation brainwashing about rape culture and feminism. But nothing that will seriously skew them towards hating men. However, if you major in the humanities or liberal arts, you are guaranteed to be thoroughly indoctrinated in leftist, socialist political propaganda, a large part of which will be feminism. Worse, you can actually major in simply "being a woman" through Women's Studies programs where all it will be is a four to eight year program in "Why Men Suck and Victimhood" studies.

Unfortunately, these degrees taint most women as most women major in the liberal arts and humanities. And any woman who joins the cult of Women's Studies is guaranteed to be completely corrupted. But, again, like politics, the level of corruption depends on how far the women take it. If you have Suzie Q who majored in "Communications," no doubt she has been fully steeped in feminism, socialism, and victimhood ideology. But she then enters the real world, works as a barista to pay back her student loans, finds out nothing she was taught has any bearing or value in the real world, and slowly becomes just another "nice, female democrat." She lands a job at the local school district, works with kids, slowly admits she likes men, and marries "Bob the Accountant." Again, not a male-hating, seething social justice warrior, but a liberal arts major nonetheless.

On the other extreme you have rank feminists who will no doubt inform you of such. They doubled down on their worthless degrees, getting masters or doctorates in these jokes of fields, and all they can do is simply reteach the same hate and invective they were taught before. This condemns them to work in college and academia their entire lives because nobody else will have them, except non-profits who might hire them as activists. You'll know to avoid these women because they'll make it hard not to, as they'll be shoving their feminist resumes and credentials in your face. But realize they still pose a threat as they account for the majority of weaponized women. You don't have to have interacted with them at all in the past as it's not beyond them to simply make up lies about you to advance their political goals. So ensure you have NOTHING to do with these women.

The tricky area is the area in between: women who may not be full blown, weaponized, male-hating feminists, but they do hold onto feminism as a quasi-religion. They aren't a "Gender Studies professor," calling for the castration of men, but they still identify as feminists and at their core believe in the victim-oppressor dichotomy. They might work as a teacher, a counselor, a social worker, or some other government or non-profit profession. Another tell is how they prioritize their careers, money, and education above love, family, husband, children, even fun. They will admit to wanting to get married "someday," but their actions indicate otherwise. One should also tread cautiously around these women.

Regardless of where women inevitably end on this spectrum, a degree in the liberal arts or humanities is a bad sign. A woman with this type of degree HAS BEEN indoctrinated in feminism and the collegiate feminist forces that be have attempted to weaponize her. Whether they were successful will require you spend more time trying to get to know that individual woman. Regardless, a worthless degree is another warning sign you should be wary of.

Bad Girls

The original Pence Principle could be more simply boiled down to "avoid the bad girls." Who are the "bad girls?" Well girls who are bad and will get you in trouble. Girls your mother warned you about.

Party girls who get drunk and make rape accusations.
Very pretty girls who are so spoiled by society they think laws, ethics, or morality don't apply to them.
Drama queens who need a constant fix of drama and chaos surrounding them.
Girls who are throwing up on the streets in the night club district at 2AM.
And attention whores who we've delved into detail before.

You know EXACTLY the type of girls we're talking about. They're the reason the Hot Crazy Matrix was created and for good reason. The real issue is whether you can have your large brain override your small one and let these succubae be.

Dating

Now that you've screened out women, in theory you can safely start dating. But don't assume just because you're dating a girl who says she's a conservative or happens to be a computer engineer that you're in the clear. Weaponized women only tend to be leftists and feminists. Plus, you might find this shocking, but sometimes women lie about who they are to get what they want. This calls for some policies and rules to follow while dating to ensure the girl you're dating is trustworthy and isn't going to accuse you of rape 36 years from now.

First, since dating is a younger man's game, this does not bode well for younger men. Because as time has gone on, each successive generation of women has become increasingly fragile, easily offended, and prone to view themselves as a victim. The incident at Facebook where hundreds of Facebook employees complained that Joel Kaplan partook in politics in his own personal time is the perfect example of precious, weaponized snowflakes overstepping their boundaries, and highlights why dating is a risky venture for young men today. Worse, many young women today think they are worthless or have no value unless they have some kind of political cause at their core. A woman today cannot simply be a good programmer, a good accountant, or a good mom. She has to be a good programmer AND be for the environment. She has to be a good accountant AND a good feminist. She has to be a good mom AND be for social justice. This bizarre and unfortunate addiction to leftist politics as well as their hyper-sensitivity, has made most young women a drastically higher risk group to date than their older contemporaries. So if you are a younger man, be acutely aware of this higher risk pool you're dating.

Second, save all texts, Facebook messages, Twitter messages, e-mails or any other form of recordable communications. More than one man has been reprieved from a false accusation of rape by showing a jury or committee texts from his accuser where she was still referring to him fondly and asking him to have sex again *after* the supposed rape happened. It is also recommended that after a date, whether there was sex or not, you get a confirmation text where you say, "Hey, how are you doing, good-lookin?" and she replies in a positive tone, proving whatever happened on the date was consensual.

Third, record your dates and any romantic interactions with women, especially when you are just starting to date. Here you'll want to consult the law in your local state a bit before doing this, but if legal it might be a good policy to always have a voice recorder recording every interaction on your person. You may also want to wear a discreet bodycam to record any events that might happen.

The initial reaction to this may be that it's overkill, but you need to consider what could happen if you're falsely accused of rape. Imagine how much pain and agony Kavanaugh would have saved had the technology existed to cheaply and easily record his interaction that didn't happen with Blasey-Ford in 1847. Imagine if Mr. Ghomeshi had a body cam on him at all times that would have allowed him to avoid the two year witch hunt and court case he went through. And imagine if Counts and Perry had a video record of what happened the night they were accused. They would have avoided 10 and 26 years in jail, respectively. Soon a $400 bodycam and getting into the habit of "hitting the record button" doesn't seem like such a chore now does it? Besides, today's technology is cheap and easy enough to use that this is not the chore it once was. And you needn't record everything all the time, but you should have the option to in the case a situation goes south or gets hairy. Every man can do this and they should. It's very cheap insurance.

Fourth, be bold, upfront, and unapologetic about it. If you tell a weaponized woman up front that you record all your dates, you have a bodycam, and, should it come to it, you will require she sign a sexual release form if you are going to have sex, she is not going to mess with you. Chances are she'll act appalled and offended and end the date.

Fine. Good riddance.

A woman who actually likes you will be shocked, but curious. She'll ask why and you can simply say the truth. "I follow the Pence Principle. I'm not ever going to get falsely accused of rape or sexual assault. I've invested too much in my life and future to have it ruined by some crazy woman who hates men or has some mental disorder. And not to accuse you of that, but until I get to know you better, I cannot take any chances." If anything it will pique her interests and actually make for a better and more honest date. It will also command respect from her if you stick to your guns and stand by such a seemingly drastic position.

Doing this will also have a secondary fringe benefit in that if enough men did this it would send a very powerful and clear message to women that enough is enough. It will show them that fake accusations are common enough that men have to resort to this level of protection, and that might get women to police their own. Many women still like men and want them to be part of their lives. And if they're shown how feminists and weaponized women are scaring men away from women, perhaps permanently, they may realize feminism for what it truly is and wage a war against it.

Fifth, the sexual consent release form. Again, 10% for shock value and to make a point, 90% for CYA, it only serves your best interest to have a stack of sexual consent release forms next to your bed (or a sexual consent app on your phone). Again, it's sterile. Again, it's inhuman. But this is the new world weaponized women and feminism has forced upon us (It's also effectively required in the state of California if you're on a college campus). If you require a woman to sign a sexual consent form, it's going to prove to her that you are deadly serious about this, and it is going to make her think, "My god, has feminism come to this?" You also may be concerned that this might ruin the mood or lessen your chances of having sex, but I think such fears are unfounded (and sadly, because of the risks, moot). Furthermore, this isn't for every time you have sex with a woman. Just until you know you can trust her and a trusting relationship has formed. But while you're out there playing the field, sowing your wild oats, it would be wise to follow a policy of CYA.

Sixth, no sex if there's alcohol.

Evidence that feminists and weaponized women are trying to expand what is considered a sexual crime can be seen with the new insistence that if a woman has had alcohol she cannot legally consent to sex. Men can drink all they want and are still responsible for giving consent. Both men and women can drink and should they drive, the police are going to rather insist you're responsible for DUI. But when it comes to sex, alcohol absolves women of all responsibilities and the ability to give consent.

There is, however, some legitimate reasoning to these laws. If a woman is completely wasted, passed out, or drugged in some other capacity, obviously it is rape and/or sexual assault. But it's the gray area that weaponized women will use to their advantage and claim that what was once tipsy consensual sex last night, is a sober rape charge the next day.

So how much alcohol is too much?

That's the gray area problem right there.

And given the gravity of the risks involved, the answer today is "any."

Unfortunately, though alcohol has been used as the social lubricant that has resulted in half the population being born today, today it's enough of an excuse to land you in jail. Until you have dated a girl long enough to trust her, it's just safe to make sure your first few sexual encounters are without booze. And if the girl wants to have sex, but has had a drink, you simply tell her in a very Pence-like way "Sorry, I don't sleep with a girl if she's had something to drink." The look on her face will be priceless, but it is almost a guarantee your rebuke will have her calling you the very next day.

Seventh, Google search the hell out of any prospective girl you might date or have sex with.

There's enough information on the internet, social media, and search engines that you should be able to find out if she's honest and trustworthy or a feminist ideologue who is looking for a fight. It may not be something political you unearth that is a deal breaker. It could be a criminal record. It could be she has a kid she forgot to mention. It could be she has a husband she forgot to mention! It's absolutely worth two hours of your time to cyberstalk your prospective dates before committing considerably more time and resources dating them.

Eighth, you are going to date crazy. You are going to call the cops.

It is a guarantee that no matter how well you screen (or how well you don't), you are going to date at least one crazy girl. Every man does. It's just a fact of life. Whether she slashes your tires, tells you "nobody puts baby in the corner," stalks you at work, or shows up at your apartment at 4AM drunk and yelling in the street, *every man is going to date at least one crazy girl.*

Recognize when you need to call the cops.

Not because you want to press charges (though, that may be the case), but in anticipation she is going to go crazy when you break up with her and will either hit you, hit herself, go crazy, and call the cops herself. The second she assaults you or your property, no matter how minor the damage, you need to contact the cops so there is a record that you contacted them first, YOU are the victim, and that woman is crazy. Unfortunately, it's more likely you're going to have three or four crazy girls in your life, if you're younger maybe seven or eight. Regardless, do not simply slough it off if a girl hits you. Contact the cops immediately because the story will soon be you hit her.

Finally, acknowledge how ugly you are and do not hit on girls 2 points higher than you. This is important because often the difference between a "charming flirtation" and "some creep harassing me" is three points on a scale of one through ten. If you're Chris Pratt and you approach a girl who's an 8, you could say "I'd like to take you home and do things to you" and she will likely go home with you and let you do things to her. But if you're Bucktooth Billy and you're a 4 and you go to that exact same girl with that exact same line, it is a guarantee you will land in jail. Know how good looking or ugly you are and do not try to punch too far above your weight.

College

At one time college was supposed to be an intellectually rewarding and fun place. America's brightest were sent off to college to help lead, evolve, and advance America and its economy. Future innovators, creators, and leaders went there to cut their teeth, learn their skills, and make their mark in society. Today, college is a joke. College has fallen greatly from its once respectable heights as nearly everybody attends, nobody is special, your professors are idiots, it's horrifically overpriced, and today's college degrees are no more valuable than a 1960's high school diploma.

Still, college holds some remnants of magic and hope, as it's the first time many people will leave home and live the life of an independent adult. It is also a time to have fun, party, and make life-long friends. But for men college holds a special place in their hearts. Because now free of their parental and high school shackles, they can pursue something that is much more important than the college education itself – girls. And here is where the trouble begins.

If you didn't notice in the previous chapters, nearly every false rape accusation we cited was made by female college students. And if you also didn't notice, they all ended badly for the accused even if they were found to be innocent. They were kicked out of school, they lost their scholarships, they were hated on campus, and they suffered an enormous psychological toll. And while it is a biological fact at 18 your sex drives are at the highest they will ever be, that is **PRECISELY** what makes college the most dangerous place for men when it comes to being attacked by weaponized women. And since your little head is likely going to be overriding your big head during these years, you really need to be careful in college.

First, the Women's Studies Department is going to start scaring all the freshmen girls on campus with bogus rape statistics. Some will say 1 in 5, others will say 1 in 3. I'm sure by now it's 1 in 1. Regardless of the actual number, campus feminists will immediately use women's worst fear to convince them they are under threat, they are victims, and you and every other man on campus are potential rapists. They want to alienate women from you, and they will.

Second, your school will further this indoctrination with "Freshman Orientation." In my day Freshman Orientation was "here's the pool, here's the gym, football field is that way, and the finance office is over there." Today it is simply more leftist indoctrination, which includes more bogus campus rape statistics, how men are all potential rapists, how men have privilege, and how women should report anything and everything because they are all victims.

Third, nearly all of your liberal arts and humanities pre-requisite classes are also going to be politically motivated. Once again, women will be constantly reminded they are oppressed, men are the oppressors, and there's a rapist behind every bush. It could be your sociology class, your political science class, even your mandatory freshman comp class. Your professors are all programmed to promote the feminist victim narrative, and this narrative will continue throughout all of a woman's college education.

I would like to say that the majority of female students are smart enough to see through this brainwashing and propaganda, but they won't. Keep in mind the indoctrination started back in grade school when Hunter Yelton got busted for sexual harassment in the 3rd grade, and the propaganda was only turned up as you marched towards your senior year. Most women will at some level believe this propaganda, and if you don't believe that simply look at the political affiliation of college age women, as well as what percent of them identify as feminists. And if that still doesn't convince you, merely pick up a copy of your local college newspaper and read any editorial about dating, rape, sex, sexual assault, feminism, or sexual harassment. It will become very clear where the political needle lies on your college campus.

Still (and it gets tiresome saying this, but it needs to be said) just because these girls happen to be democrats or feminists doesn't mean they are weaponized women. But realize and acknowledge you will never have a higher concentration of weaponized women in your life than when you are in college. You are behind enemy lines and better act as such. This means you should follow some key rules or perhaps reconsider your college education strategy in its entirety.

Rule # 1 – You are there to go to school.

You are attending college to get your education. Period. Get your education. Get your degree. Get your transcripts, and then get the hell out. Yes, college life is supposed to include rowdy parties and getting laid and getting drunk, and

I'm not saying not to cautiously participate in those things. But once you've been to one college party, you've been to them all. You're not there to party, you're not there to get laid, you're there to get an education so you can have a great career. Do not lose focus of that.

Rule # 2 – Consider getting an education online

In order for you to be falsely accused of any crime, you need to be physically near your accuser. This is not possible if you're attending school online. While it wasn't an option in the past, there are accredited programs being offered online by different colleges. You can take classes from the convenience of your own home. You don't have to commute or pay for parking. They're typically a fraction of the cost of a physical college. And there's no chance you will be accused of sexual harassment or assault because you weren't there. There was no "there" to be at. And if online schools do not appeal to you, you can consider community colleges or commuter colleges where the study body is a bit more professional, mature, and apolitical. These are not your massive four year party schools where false harassment accusations are as common as beer pong, and they are also typically cheaper than most main campus colleges.

The only problem is that many of you are young and your true motive to go to college is to party. You can lie to your parents or you can lie to yourself and say it's for an education. But that is a bold faced lie and you know it. You're going there to party and to meet girls, so you have absolutely no interest in online colleges or commuter colleges, no matter how much cheaper and safer they'd be.

But let me plant a little thought in your mind.

You are guaranteed to have the college experience regardless. The reason why is that whether you attend college or not, you're still going to go to house parties, you're still going to get drunk, you're still going to get shot down by girls, and you're still going to get lucky and get laid once a blue moon. You don't need to be plopping down $30,000 a year to attend some party school to do that. The "college experience" is simply called "your late teens and early 20's." Spare yourself the unnecessary student loan burden and higher risk of a false accusation and go to a cheap online or community college instead.

Rule #3 – Date off campus

Though not a guarantee, it might be wise to follow the rule of "Do not defecate where you eat." School is meant to be school. You're technically not really there to date or get laid. You're there to get an education. And why complicate your college life by dating and then breaking up with a score of girls all of whom you might awkwardly see on campus? Who needs the distraction? Who needs the drama? Let your college campus remain a pure place of study and date girls from other colleges or (better yet) girls who have jobs in the real world.

There is an additional benefit to this policy. You may have noticed that instead of going to the police, nearly all of the women who made false rape claims went to the college administration to report the rape instead. This is because of a federal civil rights law called "Title IX." The short version is that this law compels colleges and universities to investigate claims of sexual harassment, assault, and rape. You might ask if colleges and universities can throw you in jail or charge you with a crime. They can't. But they can kick you out of school, withdraw your scholarships, kick you out of any sports you belong to, and bring your educational career to an abrupt end. Worse, and you saw this in all the false campus rape accusations, even if you're proven innocent, you don't get your scholarships reinstated or get let back on the baseball team or even get let back into college. Furthermore, colleges and universities have no legal authority to arrest or sentence women who make false rape accusations, police do. So if a weaponized woman on campus wants to ruin you, but at no risk to herself, she can report you to the university and not the cops.

But if you're dating a girl who doesn't go to your college, she can still go to your college administration and file a false report (nothing's stopping her), but chances are it won't dawn on her to do so. She will erroneously assume her only option is to go to the cops which is much more daunting and will deter a lot of false rape and assault accusations.

Rule #4 – Date STEM, Nursing, Pre-Med, or Accounting Majors

Nothing is going to stop you men from dating when you're in college. And while it's Pence Principle 101 to avoid dating feminists, Women's Studies majors, Gender Studies majors, Sociology majors, and the like, you'll do yourself a favor by dating some of the higher quality girls. These higher quality girls are the ones pursuing higher quality degrees. Engineering, Physics, Computer Science, Accounting, Actuarial Science, Statistics, any rigorous discipline with a real career at the end of it. There's no guarantee the Chemical Engineering major you took out Saturday won't drag you in front of some kangaroo Title IX court at your college, but the risks are drastically lower when you're dating real women with real degrees. Also, they tend to be smarter and nicer than their liberal arts majoring sisters, so do yourself a favor and date girls who are lower risk and higher quality.

Work

Work is one of those places where you follow the original Pence Principle to the letter. You do not meet alone with any other woman without the presence of your wife. And you do not attend company parties where alcohol is being served without your wife. This will prevent the majority of any work-related accusations coming your way. However, realize feminists, weaponized women, and especially HR professionals look at the workplace as a hotly contested battleground to fight against "sexism, harassment, and hostile work environments." Many of them also look at it as a place to advance women over men. So some tweaks and adjustments as well as some preventative measures are needed to make your work life bulletproof against weaponized women, vindictive HR professionals, and false accusations.

First, even if it is allowed, you do not date at work. You do not defecate where you eat. You do not throw trash in your own yard. Work should be kept completely separate from your love life as it is a vital part of your life.

That needs to be restated again because it is very important.

WORK IS A VITAL PART OF YOUR LIFE.

Without work you cannot do fun things in life like eat, have shelter, have health insurance, or just plain live. If you threaten your job with an office romance you now directly threaten your life, all because Bambi in accounting batted her eyes at you. So if you like to eat, enjoy having a roof over your head, and maybe like having health insurance

You go to work.
You do your job.
You make your money.
You shut up.
And you go home.

There are plenty of girls to chase outside work.

Second, keep work and pleasure separate. Do not attend company parties. Do not attend company functions. And certainly do not attend them if there is booze involved. These people are you co-workers not your friends. There is this weird culture and push where careerists and people with no social lives use the workplace as a poor substitute for a social life, even a surrogate family. Not that there aren't friendly people at work, or that friendships won't form, but you should not make work the primary source of your social life because it complicates this vitally important part of your life. Again, think like an actuary and lower your risks of getting falsely accused. Thank your boss for the invite to the booze bash company Christmas party, but politely decline as you spend that time with real friends and a real family.

Three, do not be left alone with women. Be it your office, your cubicle, an unattended meeting room, or a conference booth, you do not spend time alone with female co-workers. You do not get donuts for the office with Suzie, you do not get lunch with Jessica, and you sure as hell do not go on business trips alone with Bambi.

Four, while it's likely impossible to never be alone with a woman over the course of your career, revert back to the tactics listed in the dating segment of this handbook. Always record conversations you have in your office. Have a discreetly placed bodycam on your person. And always save every and all electronic communications you have at work.

Five, do not say anything about your "Pence Policy." If you do, it will be a lightning rod for criticism, accusations of sexism, and will make you a target for the petty office politics of the women at the office. If you're in the meeting room by yourself and a woman walks in, you politely excuse yourself to the bathroom. If your boss says you're going to travel to Macon with Jessica for the afternoon, you agree, but then grab your boss's ear privately and tell him that you're not comfortable traveling alone with Jessica. And if you're asked to get donuts with Leslie, volunteer to do it by yourself. You essentially want to minimize yourself to the smallest presence possible, making no waves, rocking no boats, but also limiting your exposure to women. Go to work, keep your head down, be polite, quiet, and civil, avoid women, clock out at 5PM and go home.

Six, work from home if possible. Like attending school online you eliminate any chance of a fake accusation if you physically remove yourself from any accusers. It saves you money, it saves you time, it saves you gas, and it can save your career.

Finally, self-employment. As the workplace becomes increasingly politicized, and as affirmative action promotes women over better-qualified men, you'll have to ask yourself if it's worth investing this much time and effort into a risky and unmerocratic environment. You worked hard to be the best at what you did, and you should be rewarded for it. But if somebody is going to get promoted over you because that person has a vagina, your efforts would be better rewarded elsewhere. Additionally, as younger, more easily-offended, and indoctrinated women enter the work force, your chances of getting dragged in front of HR and escorted out of the building by security on some "hostile work environment charge" is only going to go up. Worse, as the Snowflake Hitlers at Facebook showed us, your personal life is their own and if they don't approve of what you're doing outside of work, they will try to get you fired. The only solution to all of this is self-employment.

For other reasons I believe the future for successful people is self-employment and not working at an increasingly Orwellian and stagnating Corporate America. But if you really want to proof yourself against false accusations of weaponized women, it's very simple. Become self-employed. If you're self-employed you can largely avoid the risks of getting falsely accused. You can work as a solo independent contractor. You can outsource work to remote companies. If you do it right, you will be a company of one and nobody will be able to file a harassment complaint against you. And even if they do, it won't matter. You're the boss and you're not going to fire yourself.

Use a Social Alias

If you want to get paid at work, you need to be you. Your employer needs your real name and social security number; otherwise you're not going to get paid.

If you want to get an education at school, you need to be you. Your college needs your real name and other identification; otherwise you're not going to get your degree and won't be able to have a productive career.

But outside those two things, you can be whoever you want. And it might prove worthwhile to go by an alias.

There are many benefits and reasons to go by a social alias. First, it will provide an additional layer of separation, keeping your personal life separate from your professional and educational lives. This will allow you to have a truly private life without tyrants and weaponized women at work holding your career hostage if you don't do what they approve of in your personal life. Imagine if Joel Kaplan had gone by "Benny Fitz" in his non-Facebook life instead.

"Why that isn't 'Joel Kaplan,' that's 'Benny Fitz.' A surprisingly similar looking doppelganger who's supporting Brett Kavanaugh, but is definitely NOT the Facebook executive!"

Second, it provides protection the other way. If you accidentally date or get involved with a weaponized woman in your private life, your working life is protected. She's not going to be able to go after your employer, stalk you, doxx you, or file a Title IX complaint because she doesn't know who your employer is, where you live, or where you go to college because she has the completely wrong name. This pre-supposes you keep other identifying information from her such as a license plate, your home address, a traceable phone number, and other bits of information that will give your identity away. But you can easily date under an alias for a long enough time to determine whether a girl is trustworthy or not to know your true identity.

Third, there is also protection on the internet and social media if you go by an alias. Using an avatar instead of a real picture and posting under a different name, you can still participate in the online political process if you want. This would be common sense, regardless of whether you choose to have an alias in your personal life, but still, do not ever use your real name or face on the internet if you're going to participate in non-left leaning politics. This will prevent you from being doxxed, getting fired for your political views, and will make your professional life all that much easier.

Finally, using a consistent social alias has the added benefit of protecting you in the future from false accusations akin to Mrs. Ford's. If the majority of the socializing you did during your youth was under "Benny Fitz," but 36 years later you're about to get promoted to CEO of Apple under your real name of "John Jones," chances are any women you may have scorned as "Benny" won't recognize you because your face has changed significantly over those 36 years. This protects you from any women who want their pound of flesh for you breaking up with them in 1992 and are willing to claim it was rape instead.

Conversely, say a weaponized woman you never knew doesn't want you to get promoted to the CEO of Apple and says, "In 1998 a drunk John Jones felt my boobies at a party." Your lawyer can interrogate her and say, "It was *John Jones*? You knew him as that then? *John Jones?* You called him *John*?" Upon which when she says, "yes," your lawyer simply points out that that's not possible, for you were never known as John Jones in 1998. You were only known as Benny Fitz.

There are some drawbacks to keeping up a social alias. You need to be consistent and present yourself socially, both in person and online, as "Benny Fitz." You have to go by an alias long enough that the majority of your friends know you as "Benny." You have to have a burner phone and phone number, as well as take measures to prevent women from seeing information that would give your real identity away (license plate, home address, etcetera). You have to create a false job, career, and education so as to protect your real career. And you have to keep up this façade until you know you can trust a woman with the truth. And even then, you'll still want to go by Benny Fitz. Keep in mind this doesn't mean you're a separate person, leading a fake life. You're still you, you still have your job, you still have your life, and you still have your hobbies. It's just that your nick name is Benny Fitz. And if all of this seems a bit much, remember that it's feminists, professional victims, and weaponized women that have made such a ludicrous thing a viable and contemplatable option.

Defending Against Lies

Finally, the hardest thing to protect against – lies.

Lies are so hard to protect against simply because they're lies. There doesn't need to be any proof. There doesn't need to be any evidence. Half the US population will believe you because "believe women." And the Democrat Party has proven it will go after and ruin the lives of private citizens even if they have to lie. Worse, the Democrat Party, feminists, and weaponized women, have also shown they're willing to go back 36 years to make an accusation, making it doubly hard, if not impossible to prove or disprove the lie. This type of fake accusation is almost impossible to protect against, and for many men that may be the case because they are too old and the means to protect their reputation from 36 years ago simply did not exist. But going forward there are some things men can do today to protect them now and into the future against any future lies that await them.

Namely, every man today is going to want to form a life-long digital alias. This is increasingly possible because of cell phones and how cellular companies track each phone. Whether you realize it or not, ever since you've had a cell phone connected to your name, you have had a digital alias recorded at the cell companies you've used over the years. There is a record of each cell phone tower your phone was reaching out to and connected to, providing a map of where you've been and where you've gone, likely for decades. This may seem a bit creepy, but it also provides a potential lifelong and life-saving alibi by being able to prove you were at certain places at certain times, refuting any false accusations claiming otherwise.

This cell phone alibi is certainly helpful, but you shouldn't rely solely on a cell phone company's records. As mentioned before you should save all your e-mails, texts, messages, and any other forms of electronic communications. You may also want to back them up physically and on the cloud. And getting a copy of your cell phone provider's cell tower records of your phone would be a wise move. In short, nearly every conversation you have today leaves some kind of digital trace or record. And if you save these records, no matter how cumbersome that might be, it provides you a lifelong record that might exonerate you from a false claim whether it's next week or when you run for congress in 2044. Again, saving a digital record of every conversation you have may seem a tedious chore. But in simply archiving your e-mails, archiving your texts, or just not hitting the "delete" button, you provide yourself with a very good insurance policy against weaponized women for the rest of your life.

CHAPTER 4
THE SAD NEW NORMAL

It is impossible to measure, but if I was forced to estimate the distribution of the current American female population today it would be a third are traditional, another third are compromised, but not weaponized, and a final third are near or fully weaponized. I would also add the younger the woman, the more thoroughly inculcated in feminist and victimhood thought she is, and therefore is more likely to be weaponized. Some of this is corroborated based on polling data as to the percent of women who identify as feminist. Some of it is based on the percent of women who believed Kavanaugh vs. Ford. Some of it is based on the statistics of women's political affiliation. And some of it is based on anecdotal experience; watching and witnessing the behaviors, beliefs, and actions of women. It is certainly up for debate, but if there was a way for this to be known the statistics would likely ballpark around at a third, a third, and a third.

These percentages will change for the worse in the foreseeable future as feminism and feminists still occupy their enviable and powerful monopoly in the education industry. Additionally, there is a nationwide craze to celebrate girls, women, and feminism that will reinforce this trend. The public schools constantly celebrate and champion girls over boys. Companies and advertisers cannot help but use feminism and "Girl Power" to separate unsuspecting young girls and women from their money. Corporations constantly celebrate "women in the workplace" and try to "empower" them through various outreach programs and initiatives. And television, media, and the movie industry condescendingly pander to women reinforcing the strong, sassy, independent, feminist stereotype. This is all fine and well if it encourages girls and emboldens them to achieve and succeed in life. Unfortunately, on the flip side of this propagandist coin is guaranteed to be victimhood politics, the "us vs. them" mentality, and often times the vilification of men. All these forces combined will shift a higher percent of the female population towards the weaponized end of the spectrum, where in 10-15 years' time you can expect 40% to be fully weaponized, 40% partially compromised, and only 20% remaining traditional.

Consequences

On the face of it, women (and men) will believe this movement is for equality, progress, and the overall advancement of society. What they won't see are some unintended and unconscious consequences. Namely, in women's pursuit to become men, they will lose their femininity and they will functionally cease to be women. This will fundamentally change society since it was built upon two distinct and separate sexes with two distinct, separate, and vital societal roles. And while most women today want nothing more than to "tear down traditional sex roles," they don't realize how this will reverberate negatively throughout the pillars of society.

First, as women are conditioned to replace family, love, husbands, and children with careers, political religions, and victimhood ideology, they are guaranteed to become more miserable. This is not even up for debate as happiness surveys show women have become increasingly less happy since the 1970's in spite of technological advances, economic growth, and nearly every 60's feminist wish list coming true. In nearly every article written about this phenomenon, the authors cite increasing sexism and discrimination in the workplace (and society) as the primary causes of this unhappiness. But a more commonsensical explanation would be that work sucks, and the more you do of it the less happy you're going to be. You don't need a doctorate in sociology to figure that out. But there is also the possibility that as women have abandoned the roles they've been programmed to play in society over the past two million years (replacing them with new ones in an evolutionary blink of an eye) this might cause some mental friction and cognitive dissonance, which might also make them unhappy. Because of the politically-incorrect nature of this ~~reality~~ theory, it's immediately dismissed as sexist or misogynist, but men aren't the ones becoming less happy over time.

Second, as society places more value on a woman's education and career than being a wife or mother, this means more education will be required to propel women to the heights of men, and perhaps beyond. Feminists, socialists, and the Democrat Party are only going to encourage this, as it benefits them politically and financially. But will it benefit women the same? College degrees are not only increasingly expensive, they're increasingly worthless. Unless women major in real fields with real jobs at the end of them, they're not only wasting their time, but incredible amounts of money. Worse, for most of the fields women choose to study, they need to get a masters or doctorate to make it pay, and even then the pay isn't that good. The end result is that millions of women will impair their financial lives for decades, arguably forever, with $50K, $100k, even $200k in student loans, with "careers" that are simply incapable of generating the income to pay said debts back. This financial ruination will not only add incredible stress to their lives, but will ironically have been caused by those who claimed to want to help out women the most – feminists, leftists and the Democrat Party.

Third, these two aforementioned consequences combined will have a devastating effect on family formation and birthing rates. With women putting careerism over love, and going into crippling levels of debt to do so, they effectively and voluntarily remove themselves from the marriage market. Not only do they personally want to postpone marriage, but by taking on such incredible levels of debt, they deter most quality men from matrimonially pursuing them in the first place. And it's not so much that these trends "will" have an effect on family formation - they already have. Women hold the majority of student loans as well as worthless degrees. The wage gap has definitely not closed. Divorce is now as common as marriage. The birthing rate has declined below sustainability levels. And what woman today bothers raising her own kids? Kids need to be shipped out to complete strangers at daycare and school so mommy can pursue her oh-so-important non-profit career. This death of the nuclear family will continue and dysfunctional, broken homes will become the norm. And any unfortunate children born into this environment will be inadequately reared, contributing to the epidemic of "ADD" and "social anxiety" type mental disorders we see in children today.

Fourth, one cannot forget what living in this feminist echo-chamber, from;

five years old in kindergarten to
25 years old in grad school to
35 years old watching re-runs of Sex and the City

will do to women's view of men over the long run. Once again, couched in the "us vs. them" dichotomy that feminism sells and today's society reinforces, increasing numbers of women will view men as the enemy, as the oppressor, and will be increasingly prone to take their personal miseries, frustrations, and failures out on them because "sexism." Additionally, with feminists and weaponized women constantly redefining and increasing what constitutes "assault," "harassment," and "rape," more and more innocent male behavior will be criminalized or at least punished socially. It will get so bad that the temper-tantrum the Little Hitlers at Facebook threw over Joel Kaplan will become commonplace. Women will feel entitled to report a man who dared to participate in politics they disagreed with in his personal life, viewing it as a fireable offense. More and more men will be falsely accused by more and more weaponized women of more and more petty, innocent things, to the point the sexes will be unable to work with one another, and every interaction will have to be chaperoned and codified.

Fifth, trust between the sexes will collapse, or at least decay. With an increasing number and severity of false accusations against men, men are going to increasingly distrust women. This may result in more men following a Pence Principle at work, but it will manifest itself more so in the fact that employers will hire women, but not trust them. This is already happening in that, if you think about it, mandatory sexual harassment training is not done so that women have a "safe and comfortable place to work." It's done in the anticipation that if a woman files a sexual harassment complaint against a co-worker, the company has a perfectly good legal defense in case they get sued in that they did their due diligence. It's simple CYA. In other words, the relationship between the sexes will become so adversarial and so risky that institutions within America will have to codify how the two sexes can interact, yet still function within the institution. Schools, colleges, universities, employers, corporations, governments, non-profits, meetup groups, and even social clubs will have to baby sit full grown adult men and women to make sure women are not offended, harassed, or even slightly peeved - not because they care about women, but because they're afraid they'll get sued. This will render nearly all institutions in America impossible places to work and conduct business, slowing economic growth, and resulting in a slow, but consistent exodus of men from corporate America into either the harsher (though safer) trades or remote work careers.

Sixth, men and women will become increasingly less human and more roboticized over time. With more distrust sown between the sexes, and male and female interaction increasingly codified, babysat, and controlled, what once came natural and was fun, will be deterred, punished, and deemed too risky. Instead of passionately and courageously (though perhaps awkwardly and drunkenly) approaching a woman in person, men will "swipe right" if they date at all, more likely opting for porn because it's easier and risk free. Women, however, will have their own special hell to contend with as they are conflicted into paralysis. On the feminist one hand they don't need men, but on the genetic other hand, they really want one. On the feminist one hand, men are the enemy, but on the genetic other hand, there's this really nice, hot guy called "Steve." On the feminist one hand, you have the power and right to ask out Steve, but on the genetic other hand not one girl in the history of "strong, empowered women" ever built up the courage to actually be equal and ask out a man. In the end, most men will lose the most important thing in their lives and women theirs. Love will be the exception, not the rule. Careers will replace families. Politics will replace happiness. And everybody's life will be unbelievably unfulfilled

But thank god you will have finally made every woman a man.

"Hell Hath No Fury...Like a Miserable Feminist"

If you have not figured this out already, it's will not just men who are the victims of weaponized women. It's women themselves who will arguably suffer the most. This isn't to dismiss the pain and suffering falsely accused men like Ghomeshi, Kavanaugh, Counts, and Perry endured, nor to forgive their vile and evil false accusers. But it is to show you what happens to people when they believe and live a lie. They suffer immeasurably.

In this particular case women have been fed the lie that the most important things in their lives are their careers, politics, educations, and themselves. Their philosophies and beliefs about being a woman. How much money they make, how many degrees they have, and what politically-correct causes they support. And while there is no doubt the individual, their beliefs, and their morality can have value, infinitely more important than that is the love and compassion of others. Unfortunately, all of feminist and weaponized women's value is self-derived. Nobody confers value upon them, only themselves. And if you don't believe this, merely read any book on feminism, listen to any seminar by a feminist, or take a class on feminism and you will realize it is nothing but looking into a mirror and worshipping the image you see. Narcissus was humble compared to these people. Regardless, no matter how much feminists and weaponized women love themselves, that self-love just simply doesn't compare to the love of others.

Making matters worse for feminists and weaponized women is biology and genetics. Because while you can certainly love a friend, love a family member, or a general loved one, women are programmed by millions of years of human evolution to desire the love of a husband and children the most. Maybe not all of them, but the number one thing in life for the vast majority of women, both alive today, in the past, and into the future, is and forever-will-be the love of a husband and any would-be children. And women, feminist or not, weaponized or not, have three choices when it comes to this accepting or denying fact.

Number one, they can accept it and live in reality. If they do this, it means they have to consider what men want in terms of a wife and mother. This could be an entire essay on its own; but in short men want physical beauty, youth, fertility, and a kind, supporting demeanor. Feminists might scoff at this, saying it's sexist or demeaning, but those accusations are trumped this being a fact. This is what men want. And if you want to satisfy the most important biological drive you have in your entire DNA code, you would be wise to be beautiful, be attractive, be nice, and be selfless.

Number two, they can deny it in its entirety. This is what feminists, leftists, and weaponized women do. "They don't need no man." "Women need a man like a fish does a bicycle." You've heard the phrases before. And it would be a wonderful blessing to the rest of us if these women did what they said and went about their merry way. But as discussed in the "Body Mutilation" and "Fat Acceptance" segments of this handbook, they don't. They're still obsessed over men, because otherwise they would not make such a stink and hate about it. They would not constantly attack men and blame them for things like "privilege" or "patriarchy." They would just go and live their lives alone and leave men the same.

The third option is a hybrid and is what the "partially corrupted" third of women do today. They acknowledge they would like to get married, but place equal, if not higher value on what feminism told them they should. Careers, education, politics, etcetera are as important, if not, *more important* than getting married and having children. And this shows in their actions, as many women aren't explicitly stated feminists, but certainly are careerists.

They have to go to college to get some worthless degree they're passionate about. They have to get a masters or doctorate in the field because it doesn't pay. They then have to work some menial, low paid jobs, just to get their foot in the door. And once their career starts to gain traction, they can't take off to start a family let alone date. Besides, there's still a $79,403 balance left on their student loans. And they can't settle down now!! They're just hitting their prime!!!…at 34. So by the time they've paid off their loans, have an established career, and checked off all the boxes feminism told them to, they're 43. The tragic joke feminism and Mother Nature played on them is no man is who is serious about starting a family is going to start looking at women in their 40's. Men are most attracted to women in their 20's and biology also favors eggs of the same age.

Now there are consequences for these three choices.

The first one, where women acknowledge genetic reality and admit they want a family, will likely end in an actual family. A woman will maintain her physique and appearance enough to attract a quality man she will love. She will realize and acknowledge that this man and any kids they have will be the most important thing in her life. And in exchange for her love and support, the family will love her in return. She can still become an accountant. She can still become an engineer. She just puts the love of others over self-love, and consequently enjoys a satisfied biological drive and a much happier life.

The second one is a life of misery. Here, feminists torture themselves over the paralyzing fear of the work it would take to attract a quality man and raise a family, versus their genetic hardwiring screaming at them to do so. In being feminists, it's very clear which side they chose, but biological reality keeps eating them from the inside. And this shows in their ugly appearance and angry faces. Though this may seem a cheap shot, it is not. Merely look at how ugly and unhappy feminists look. Mrs. Ford was not happy or good-looking. Hillary Clinton, definitely not happy. Nancy Pelosi, not happy. And any women's studies department staff, ugly and not happy. They can pen thousands of books, issue millions of Women's Studies degrees, deliver tons of speeches, and talk about self-love all they want, but the permanent and miserable scowls on their faces tell the truth.

The third one is a life of confusion and betrayal. These women acknowledged they wanted to get married and have children "someday," but not at the expense of their career, politics, or education. Additionally, depending on how much cool aid they drank, they may also believe things that either won't make a family possible or will result in a dysfunctional one. A woman who values her career more than her family will likely divorce and will certainly pay someone else to raise her doomed children. A woman who thinks men are shallow for liking physically attractive women, will never hit the treadmill, never attract a man, and will never get married (or at least drive their husband into the bosom of another woman). A woman who is a careerist or obsessed about education, is in school or her career too long, losing both her beauty and fertility, only seriously hitting the marriage market as she hits menopause. Or a woman who was financially burdened with student loans for a Sociology degree deters any men because she is a financial liability. These women are not immediately angry, but grow angrier over time as what they were promised is never delivered. And this anger only gets worse as they realize their chance at true happiness was squandered long ago and can never be recovered again. In the pursuit of "having it all," they wound up with nothing

Out of these three groups, only the first one is not going to be rabidly angry at the world and men. They accepted the truth, they accepted reality, they made decisions based in both, and consequently enjoy happy (happier, technically) lives.

The remaining two groups are angry. *Very angry*. They have lost everything. Nothing they promised to themselves came to fruition. Their entire lives have been wasted. And though there is no guarantee, if you once again look at the feminist "us vs. them" dichotomy, the male-oppressor/female-victim narrative, the indoctrination that goes into women from 5 to 35, the numerous cases of false accusations cited in this handbook, not to mention the terms *"patriarchy"* and *"male privilege"*…

just who do you think they're going to blame?

These women already proved they lack the intellectual strength and courage to accept reality. Most of them have shown they are lazy as they self-centeredly chose to derive all their value through self-love and not external love, because self-love is easy and effortless, while external love is hard and difficult to earn. Most of these women consciously chose easier degrees and paths in life hoping they'd get lucky in landing some cushy government, non-profit, or academic job. And instead of working hard, learning some calculus, or maybe working on an oil rig, they constantly whine and complain about the ~~wage~~ effort gap.

You think they're all of the sudden going to take ownership of the consequences of their decisions? You damn well know they are going to blame men in one capacity or another for their failures. And whether you ever lifted a finger to oppress, hurt, assault, or even inconvenience a woman, they are coming after you. You are male, you are the enemy, you are to blame.

It is unfortunate that male-female relations have deteriorated to this level in this country. It is sad that men have been ruined for women, and women ruined for men, ruining the best things in life for both of us. But lamentable as this is, it doesn't lessen the very real threat this weaponization of women presents to men. Everything every man has worked for in his life is potentially at risk. Your education, your career, your finances, your happiness, your family, your life, and your future. You simply cannot afford to be ignorant or idealistic about what is going around you because the price is too big. Consequently and regrettably, this makes this handbook mandatory reading for every man, young or old, in America and the western world. Do not be foolish and think a false accusation won't happen to you. Assume it will and take the necessary steps to either prevent it from happening or protecting from it when it does. Please follow and practice The Pence Principle.

THE END

36782706R00080

Made in the USA
Lexington, KY
17 April 2019